SCARY VERSION *for* CHRISTIANS

THE SPIRIT OF TRUTH
WILL GUIDE YOU
INTO ALL TRUTH

RONALD F. PETERS
Missionary since 1978,
ordained minister

Note: The front cover was painted
by Ronald F. Peters, in May of 1956.

One Printers Way
Altona, MB R0G 0B0
Canada

www.friesenpress.com

First Edition — 2023

ISBN
978-1-03-918355-1 (Hardcover)
978-1-03-918354-4 (Paperback)
978-1-03-918356-8 (eBook)

1. RELIGION, CHRISTIAN THEOLOGY, ESCHATOLOGY

Distributed to the trade by The Ingram Book Company

Every country is politically under pressure today, and Christians have not offered any assistance to their governments with positive Bible information. The world is deteriorating. Wars are looming on the horizon. To criticize our leaders, makes Christians no different than the unrighteous. God considers protests in the same category as complaining. The Bible is very clear on how God handles complaining. (Numbers 12 and Numbers 14: 35-38,
And Numbers 16:30-34

Howbeit when he,
the Spirit of Truth, is come,
he will guide you into all truth:
for he shall not speak of himself;
but whatsoever he shall hear,
that shall he speak:
and he will show you things to come.
St. John 16: 13

We are on the brink of major change. Our lives will change. This book is written for Christians to prepare.

Please note: That all scripture references are taken from the "King James Authorized Version".

Table of Contents

PREFACE
The Scary Version, for Christians.

You will want to read this book,
even if you are not a Christian,
because it tells you precisely what it will be like,
for people that don't really believe in God.
It will definitely be scary for them too.
Most Christians are now looking for that quick escape
called "the rapture".
This book will show what the bible actually says.
This book will also show how,
Christians will get through the resurrection,
and exactly what that will be like.

2 Peter 3:10-11
But the day of the Lord will come as a thief in the night;
in the which the heavens shall pass away with great noise,
and the elements shall melt with fervent heat,
the earth also and the works that are therein shall be burned up.
Seeing then that all these things shall be dissolved,
what manner of persons ought ye to be
in all holy conversation and godliness.

Isaiah 34:4
And all the "host of heaven" shall be dissolved, (all those galaxies)
and the heavens shall be rolled together as a scroll:
and all their host shall fall down,
as the leaf falleth off from the vine,
and as a falling fig from the fig tree.

Note:
This book will show you truths.
But only truths that are "Bible Verses".
Not some man-made truths.
Although there will be many scary things
from now, until the end of this world,
except for the time of 666,
God has determined that Christians
will be protected during the tribulation.
Christians must not be afraid.
Not even a little bit.
Trust God.
We will be safe.

The Word of God is His Majesty "King Jesus"

Question: Is the entire Bible, Jesus Christ speaking to us ?

God says in: ***St. John 1:1-3***

In the beginning was the Word,
and the word was with God,
and the word was God.
The same was in the beginning with God.
all things were made by him;
and without him was not anything made that was made.

Question: Was this Word of God,
that made everything
actually King Jesus?

God says in: ***St. John 1:14***

And the Word was made flesh
and dwelt among us,
(and we beheld his glory, the glory as of the only begotten
of the Father,)
full of grace and truth

Question: Is this Word of God also the same King Jesus
who is coming back for us at the last day?

God says in: ***Revelation 19:11-13***

And I saw heaven opened,
and behold a white horse;
and he that sat upon him was called Faithful and True,
and in righteousness he doth judge and make war.
His eyes were a flame of fire,
and on his head were many crowns;
and he had a name written,
that no man knew,
but he himself.
And he was clothed with a vesture dipped in blood:
and his name is called "The Word of God".

Since we know that the Word of God is His majesty, King Jesus, is it important to know the amount of power that is actually in the word of God.

Hebrews 4:12
For the word of God (we are talking about the Holy Bible)
is quick,
and powerful
and sharper
than any two-edged sword,
piercing even to the dividing asunder of soul and spirit,
and of the joints and marrow,
and is a discerner of the thoughts
and intents of the heart.

Amazing: The word knows your thoughts.
The word knows the intents of your heart.

St. John 6:63

It is the Spirit that quickeneth;
the words that I speak unto you,
they are spirit,
and they are life.

CHAPTER 1
It starts with a teachable spirit

Proverbs 13:18 Poverty and shame shall be to him that refuseth instruction:
but he that regardeth reproof shall be honoured.

Proverbs 4:5
Get wisdom, (a gift of the Holy Spirit)
get understanding:
forget it not;
neither decline from the words of my mouth (hearing the voice of King Jesus)

Note:
God expects every Christian to have a teachable spirit.
Everyone needs to ask themselves: "do I have a teachable spirit".
Most Christians around the world do not have a teachable spirit.
They have learned the fundamentals of their Christianity
from whomever led them to Christianity,
and consequently they are very firm in the belief
that anything else is heresy and should be ignored and rejected.

That is why we have almost 45,000 denominations globally.
There are about 2.3 billion Christians globally.
Catholicism has about 1.345 billion.
Protestants have about one billion.
However, the actual number of major ecclesiastical traditions worldwide is about 300.

"There has never been a united Christianity".
Christians have always had diverse opinions on Christian doctrine.
But God has not, at any time, had diverse opinions.
God has been very consistent on all doctrine and theology.
God has never vacillated.
Regarding unity, there are two types of Christian unity.

Institutional unity: denominations are human institutions.

Christian unity: Does not require that we be part of the same institution.
Nor does Christian unity require that we agree on everything.
You cannot find a single church in the world where
everyone believes
exactly the same thing on every point.
The vast majority of Christian denominations
are united in a common faith in Christ.
What binds Christians together is our faith in Christ,
and our submission to Jesus.

However, God has not left theological issues to chance in his Holy Bible.
He clearly issued a statement regarding unity.

In ***Ephesians 4:13-14*** , God says:
"Till we all come in the unity of the faith,
and of the knowledge of the Son of God,
unto a perfect man,
unto the measure of the stature of the fullness of Christ:
that we henceforth be no more children,
tossed to and fro,
and carried about with every wind of doctrine,
by the sleight of men,
and cunning craftiness,
whereby they lie in wait to deceive.

Note:
It was never God's intention to have denominations.
There are not hundreds of methods to achieve salvation.
There are not hundreds of methods to live Christianity.
There are not hundreds of methods to live God's church plan.

Denominations have grown through :
- differences in belief
- corruption
- power grabs.

Ephesians 4:4
There is one body,
and one Spirit,
even as ye are called in one hope of your calling.

1 Corinthians 3:2-6
I have fed you with milk,
and not with meat:
for hitherto ye were not able to bear it,
neither yet now are ye able.
for ye are carnal:
For whereas there is among you
envying,
and strife,
and divisions,
are ye not carnal,
and walk as men?
For while one saith,
I am of Paul;
and another, I am of Apollos;
are ye not carnal?
Who then is Paul,
and who is Apollos,
but ministers by whom ye believed,
even as the Lord gave to every man.

I have planted, Apollos watered;
but God gave the increase.

Note:

Right after King Jesus left planet earth,
there were differences of opinion on doctrine.
Eventually, over the next three hundred
and fifty years,
church hierarchy was formulated.
Not the biblical hierarchy.
And it quickly evolved to power.
And the church became rich.
And the hierarchy made up their own rules and theology.
Centuries later some Christians realized they had been duped
and started their own denominations.
This quickly became a trend and over the next few decades,
Christianity became the most divided of all religions.
It's still like that. Actually, it's worse.

God had laid out his plan for Christianity at the beginning,
and it is still his plan.
God cannot vacillate.

This book will explain exactly where Christianity went wrong.

However, this book is an entire waste of time
until a church determines that they are teachable.
That means that they are willing to change.
It's a big change.
It depends entirely on how much
they actually believe the Holy Bible.
All of the Holy Bible.
It's God 's word.

A teachable spirit can receive instruction.
It can receive wisdom.
It can receive truth.

Truth is not manmade.
It is the word of God.

In ***Proverbs 8:5-10,*** God has said:

O ye Simple,
understand wisdom:
and ye fools, be ye of an understanding heart.
Hear;
for I will speak of excellent things;
and the opening of my lips shall be right things.
For my mouth shall speak truth;
and wickedness is an abomination to my lips.
All the words of my mouth are in righteousness;
there is nothing froward or perverse in them.
They are "plain to him that understandeth",
and right to them that find knowledge.
Receive my instruction,
and not silver;
and knowledge rather than gold.

God wants us to do things according to his way.

In ***Proverbs 8:32-34,*** God has said:

Now therefore hearken unto me,
O ye Children:
for blessed are they that keep
my ways.
Hear instruction,
and be wise,
and refuse it not.
Blessed is the man that heareth me,
watching daily at my gates,
waiting at the posts of my doors.

Note:
When he says: "watching daily at my gates",
it means that there is always much more to learn.
It means that people are to be
willing to learn every day,
and then willing to change
to God's ways.

If you have a teachable spirit
It means that you are going to learn things
that are different from what you have understood so far.
It may even be contrary to your current theology.
It may upset you in the beginning.
But,
if it is from the Holy Bible
and it lines up with several scriptures,
you will need to change your belief.
You need to accept that you are in learning mode
and your thinking is going to change.
God expects you to be in learning mode.
God expects you to change.
God wants to give you much more,

of things of the Holy Spirit.
God wants you to be able to operate in the Spirit.
God wants you to be involved with the gifts of the Holy Spirit.
God wants you to experience the power in the Holy Spirit.
God want you to experience the joy in the Holy Spirit.
God wants you to experience the revelations in the Holy Spirit.
God expects you to pray power prayers, in the Holy Spirit. (tongues)

There is much more to learn.
The Holy Spirit will begin to teach you !
King Solomon was given the wonderful gift of wisdom.
Then he taught us (you and me)
how to understand God's wisdom and instruction.

Proverbs 1:1-7
The proverbs of Solomon
the son of David,
King of Israel;
To know wisdom and instruction;
to perceive the words of understanding;
to receive the instruction of
wisdom,
justice,
and judgment,
and equity;
to give subtilty to the simple,
to the young man knowledge and discretion.
A wise man will hear,
and will increase learning;
and a man of understanding shall attain unto wise counsels:
to understand a proverb,
and the interpretation;
the words of the wise,
and their dark sayings.
"The fear of the Lord" is the beginning of knowledge
but fools despise wisdom and instruction.

Note:
There is very good reason to have fear
(Actually being scared)
of "His Majesty King Jesus".
Why?
Because if you don't
totally respect him,
and obey him
you lose

1. his protection
2. his blessings.

We can see everything around us,
but
what we cannot see,
is the "spirit world" around us.
This spirit world is very real.
Satan and his demons are all around us.
The agenda of these demons involves only three things:
1. To steal
2. To destroy
3. and to kill

St. John 10:10
The thief cometh not,
but for
1.to steal,
2.and to kill,
3.and to destroy:
I am come that they might have life,
and that they might have it more abundantly.
(King Jesus wants us to have life more abundantly.)

Ephesians 6:12
For we wrestle not
against flesh and blood,
but
against principalities,
against powers
against the rulers of darkness of this world,
against spiritual wickedness in high places.

2 Corinthians 11:14
And no marvel;
for Satan himself
is transformed into an angel of light.

CHAPTER 2
Six principles of the "Doctrine of Christ"

MILK

Hebrews 5:12-14

For when for the time ye ought to be teachers,

(God expects every new convert to shortly begin to teach
those that the convert has brought to Christ's salvation,
because that is by far the fastest way to learn.
The teacher always learns the most.
And that is one of the first principles of the oracles of God)

ye have need that one teach you again,
which be the first principles of the oracles of God;
and are become such as have need of milk,
and not of strong meat.
For
everyone that useth milk
is unskillful in the word of righteousness:
For he is a baby.
but
strong meat belongeth to them
that are of full age,
even those who by reason of use
have their senses exercised
to discern both good and evil.

The six milk things

Hebrews 6: 1-2
Therefore (because of the previous statements)
leaving the principles of the "Doctrines of Christ"
let us go on unto perfection;
not laying again:

1. the foundation of repentance from dead works,
2. and of faith toward God,
3. of the doctrine of Baptisms, (more than one)
4. and of laying on of hands,
5. and of resurrection of the dead,
6. and of eternal judgment.

Note:
These six principles are the "milk" that St. Paul is referring to.
St. Paul is suggesting that we should be going on to strong meat,
and be partakers of the Holy Ghost, and the power of God.
God has said that those six principles are milk,
to start a new disciple in the basics of Christ's theology.
However he refers to strong meat
which indicates that there is much more to learn.

Question: Did God talk about teaching doctrine in the old testament ?

God says in***: Isaiah 28:9-10***

> Whom shall he teach knowledge?
> and whom shall he make to understand doctrine?
> them that are weaned from the milk,
> and drawn from the breasts.
>
> For precept must be upon precept,
> Precept upon precept;
> line upon line,
> line upon line,
> here a little
> and there a little.

Most churches around the world have not learned the six milk things yet.

CHAPTER 3
Milk 1. Repentance

Psalm 51:3-4 Admitting your sin
For I acknowledge my transgressions:
and my sin is ever before me.
Against thee, thee only, have I sinned,
and done this evil in thy sight:
that thou mightiest be justified when thou speakest,
and be clear when thou judgest.

Note:
When I teach "repentance"
I often use this illustration:

One day I get tempted and steal the pastors car.
No one knows, and for a long time I get away with it.
Eventually my conscience bothers me, and I go and tell the pastor that it was me that stole his car. I admit my sin.
The pastor is shocked, but being the nice fellow that he is, he forgives me.
I thank him for forgiving me, and I go home and keep the car.

I have not done repentance.

Psalm 51:7 Purge me and wash me
Purge me with hyssop, and I shall be clean:
wash me, and I shall be whiter than snow.

Psalm 51:10 Create in me a clean heart
Create in me a clean heart,
O God
and renew a right spirit within me.
Psalm 51:11 Take not thy Holy Spirit from me
Cast me not away from thy presence.
and take not thy Holy Spirit from me.

Psalm 51:12 Restore the joy of thy Salvation
Restore unto me the joy of thy salvation;
and uphold me with thy free spirit.

Psalm 51:13-15 Commitment to servanthood
Then I will teach transgressors thy ways;
and sinners shall be converted unto thee.
Deliver me from blood guiltiness,
O God,
thou God of my salvation:
and my tongue shall sing aloud of thy righteousness.
O Lord,
open thou my lips;
and my mouth shall show forth thy praise.

All sins require repentance

There are the ten commandments. ***Exodus 20:1-17***

1. No other Gods (***Exodus 23:24-33***
   Do you know of any pastor that is
   speaking against foreigners bringing idols into our country?)
2. No graven images or any likeness of anything
3. Not take the name of the Lord our God in vain (Do you know of any pastor that speaks out against swearing)
   Levit. 24:10-16)
4. Remember the Sabbath day (do you know of a pastor who speaks against working on Sunday, or shopping or gardening)

Leviticus 19:30 keep my Sabbaths and reverence my Sanctuary
Numbers 15:32-36 he gathered sticks on the Sabbath day
Romans 14:5-6 If people do the Sabbath on a day other than Sunday, God doesn't change the rules.

5. Honour thy father and mother
6. Thou shalt not kill (**Numbers 32:23)**
7. Thou shalt not commit adultery
8. Thou shalt not steal
9. Thou shalt not bear false witness (**Leviticus 6:1-5**)
10. Thou shalt not covet.

Isaiah 59:2
But your iniquities (sins) have separated
between you and your God,
and your sins have hid his face from you,
that he will not hear.

Romans 1:26-32
For this cause God gave them up unto vile affections:
for even their women did change the natural use
into that which is against nature:
And likewise
also the men,
leaving the natural use of the woman,
burned in their lust one to another;
men with men working that which is unseemly,
and receiving in themselves that recompense of their error
which was meet. (proper, agreeable, worthy)
And
even as they did not like to retain God in their knowledge,
God gave them over to a reprobate mind,
to do those things which are not convenient;

Note:
(God was talking about the gay community in the previous verses,
and then God describes what they are now filled with.)

Being filled with all
unrighteousness,
fornication,
wickedness,
covetousness,
maliciousness;
full of envy,
murder,
debate,
deceit,
malignity,
whisperers,
backbiters,
haters of God,
despiteful,
proud,
boasters,
inventors of evil things,
disobedient to parents,
without understanding,
covenant breakers,
without natural affection,
implacable,
unmerciful:
who knowing the judgment of God,
that they which commit such things
are worthy of death,
not only do the same, (those that do the above sins)
but have pleasure in them that do them.

Note:
Having pleasure in watching people commit such things,
will result in the same punishment.

1 Corinthians 6:9-10

Know ye not
that the unrighteous
shall not inherit the kingdom of God?

Be not deceived:
neither fornicators,
nor idolaters,
nor adulterers,
nor effeminate,
nor abusers of themselves with mankind,
nor thieves,
nor covetous,
nor drunkards,
nor revilers,
nor extortioners,
shall inherit the kingdom of God.

Note:
In churches,
without some form of monitoring,
there is only sanctioning of the sins committed.
People hate some sins, like: thou shalt not kill, or steal, or covet;
but then they excuse other sins with "we are now under grace".
It's not confusing to God,
who calls sins an abomination.

Proverbs 6:16-19
These six things doth God hate:
Yea, seven are an abomination unto him:

1. a proud look,
2. a lying tongue,
3. and hands that shed innocent blood,
4. an heart that deviseth wicked imaginations,
5. feet that be swift in running to mischief,
6. a false witness that speaketh lies,
7. and he that soweth discord among brethren.

How to stop sinning.

Romans 6:16
Know ye not that to whom ye yield yourselves servants to obey,
His servants ye are to whom ye obey;
Whether of sin unto death,
Or of obedience unto righteousness.

Psalms 119:11
Thy word have I hid in my heart ,
That I might not sin against thee.

Note:
I teach people to learn one verse a week.
Write the same verse on six pieces of paper.
Small notes like a yellow sticky.

Tape these notes in obvious places:

1. Where you sit to watch TV
2. Beside you in the washroom
3. Near the kitchen table
4. On your desk at work
5. On your phone.
6. on the dashboard of you car
7. where you wash your dishes
8. on your refrigerator

Every week a new verse !
That's one hundred and four verses in two years.

God says it will help you to stop sinning !

CHAPTER 4
Milk 2. Faith

Hebrews 11:1 The definition

Now faith is the substance of things hoped for,
The evidence of things not seen.

Hebrews 11:6 Is faith optional?

But without faith
It is impossible to please him:
for he that cometh to God must believe that he is,
and that he is a rewarder
of them that diligently seek him.

Romans 10:17 How can we get faith?

So then
faith cometh by hearing,
and hearing by the word of God.

Note:

To increase your faith, you need to go to a church
that preaches the word of God.
There are two types of preachers.

- One that gives you five minutes of "word of God" and twenty minutes word of man.
- One that gives you twenty minutes of word of God and five minutes word of man.

St. Paul said:

1 Corinthians 1:18 The Power Of God
For the preaching of the cross is
to them that perish foolishness:
but
unto us which are saved
it is the power of God.

James 1:6-8 Wavering gets you nothing from God
But let him ask in faith, nothing wavering.
For he that wavereth is like a wave of the sea
driven with the wind and tossed.
For let not that man think that he shall receive anything from the Lord.
A double minded man is unstable in all his ways.

CHAPTER 5
Milk 3A - Water Baptism

King Jesus was leaving planet earth.
So he (His Majesty King Jesus) gave us his last speech,
with what he thought were the most important facts,
to explain his Christian Gospel,
to the remaining eleven disciples.

St. Mark 16:15-19
And he said unto them:
go ye into all the world,
and preach the Gospel (the message of who Jesus was before he came down
from God in heaven, to earth, to save us from our sins,
his life, his healings, and miracles,
his death, the shedding of his blood,
to wash away our sins, and his resurrection.)
to every creature.

(Then he told them "who were saved" and "who were not saved").

He that believeth and is baptized shall be saved.
but
he that believeth not shall be damned. (of course if they are not going to believe the gospel, they certainly are not going to get
water baptized either.)

(Then he told them: "this is how you can tell the believers. These are the signs of them that believe".)

And these signs shall follow them that believe;
In my name they shall

1. cast out devils;
2. they shall speak with new tongues
3. they shall take up serpents
4. and if they drink any deadly thing it shall not hurt them
5. they shall lay hands on the sick, and they shall recover.

So then after the Lord had spoken unto them,
he was received up into heaven,
and sat on the right hand of God.

Note:
Those five signs are how King Jesus described them that believe.
In most of the churches around the world,
all five of these items are missing.

Every hospital has a psych ward full of demon possessed people.
Where are the believers?
Besides God, who actually cares?
These demon possessed people in Psych wards are discarded people.
And the Christians are busy praising God that they are living in the "blessing's realm."
I visit a psychiatric hospital twice a month. The people walk around like zombies.
These people are very lonely. They are in a permanent jail.
Most of them never have a visitor.
Most of them are not able to involve in activities.
What do you think their after-life will be like? Do you know of anyone who cares?

Every Sunday in church,
I wonder why nobody knows about this.
Our hospitals are full of sick people.
Every church has people in their congregation

who need a healing.
In most churches there is no evidence of God action.
Some pray for people at the front of the church,
but no one gets healed.

The first sign that a saved person is really a believer:
is that they will be casting out devils.
I don't know of even one church where that is going on.
Warning:
Christians who have not put on the Spirit of Christ (Water Baptism into Jesus Christs Death : Galatians 3:27)
and subsequently have not received the baptism of the Holy Spirit and speaking in tongues, should not attempt to cast out devils. Without having put on Christ, the devils can resist a human.
The sons of Sceva tried and the evil spirit ripped off their clothes and wounded them.
The Acts 19: 13 -16. They thought the name of Jesus would be enough to cast out demons.

The second sign that a saved person is really a believer:
is that he will be speaking in tongues.
That is also extremely rare in most churches.

The fifth sign that a saved person is really a believer:
is that he will lay his hands on sick people, and they actually recover.
That also is very rare. And people that have this gift generally don't use it.

In the last three months I have visited three churches.
When church is finished,
I have not heard one person talking about the sermon.
I have not heard one person talking about something Christian.
I have not heard one person talking about helping a need somewhere.
I have not had one person address my salvation, even though I was a total stranger in their midst. Actually, most avoided me.

The ritual of water baptism

Most churches around the world baptize babies by hand wetting water on the top of a babies head. By this baptism, the baby has received the sacrament of regeneration and initiation into the church.

Other churches baptize adults who have understanding of the process, and walk them into water and fully immerse the candidate saying the prayer over them " I now baptize you in the name of the Father, and the Son, and the Holy Ghost.

Many protestant churches invite unsaved people to the front of the church,
and have them repeat a sinners prayer after the speaker, following which they announce that those who have repeated this prayer before God, have now been born again.

None of these three things are correct theology.

Romans 6:3-11
God has told us:
Know ye not
that as many of us as were baptized into Jesus Christ
were baptized into his death?
Therefore
we are buried with him by baptism into death:
that like as Christ was raised up from the dead
by the glory of the Father,
even so we also should walk in newness of life.
For if we have been planted together in the likeness of his death,
(that's why we need to be baptized completely under the water, planted)
we shall be also in the likeness of his resurrection:
Knowing this,
that our old man is crucified with him,
that the body of sin might be destroyed,
that henceforth we should not serve sin.
For he that is dead is freed from sin.

Now if we be dead with Christ,
we believe that we shall also live with him:
Knowing that Christ being raised from the dead dieth no more;
Death hath no more dominion over him.
For in that he died, he died unto sin once:
but in that he liveth,
he liveth unto God.
Likewise reckon ye also yourselves to be dead indeed unto sin,
but alive unto God through Jesus Christ our Lord.

Note :
Being buried with Christ into his death by baptism
that the body of sin might be destroyed,
is the purpose.
Verse seven says:
He that is dead is freed from sin.
Because we are then dead with Christ, and as in verse eight ,
we believe we shall also live with him.
Verse eleven says: likewise reckon ye yourselves to be dead indeed to sin,
but alive unto God through Jesus Christ our Lord.

This is why Jesus said to Nicodemus:
St. John 3:3
Verily, verily, I say unto thee,
except a man be born of water and of the Spirit,
he cannot enter into the Kingdom of God.

Note: What is Born Again?

So, when people say that that are "born again Christians",
it actually means, that they have been planted together
in the likeness of Christ's death.
Born again means: that they were buried by baptism into his death
and then rising out of death,
to be born again, alive unto God through Jesus Christ.
They are then "born again". But they had to die first.

Romans 6:3-4
God has said:
Know ye not,
that so many of us as were baptized into Jesus Christ
were baptized into his death?
Therefore, we are buried with him by baptism into death:
That like as Christ was raised up from the dead
by the glory of the Father,
even so we also should walk in newness of life.

Note:
It is interesting to note:
that to be baptized into Jesus Christ
results to be baptized into his death.
Not into Gods death.
Not into the Holy Spirits death.
Only into Jesus Christ's death.
Buried with him by baptism into death.
Is it necessary to be baptized completely under water?
Romans says "buried" with him by baptism.
This is why we don't say :
I baptize you in the name
of the Father,
and of the Son,
and of the Holy Ghost.
The father has never died. And the Father was never buried.
The Holy Ghost has never died. And the Holy Ghost was never buried.

Buried means completely under the water.

God tells us the story of King Jesus being baptized:
St. Matthew 3:13-17
Then cometh Jesus from Galilee to Jordan unto John,
to be baptized of him.
But John forbade him,
saying,

I have need to be baptized of thee,
and comest thou to me?
And Jesus answering said unto him,
suffer it to be now: (and now the reason)
For thus it becometh us to fulfil all righteousness.

(not just some, but all.
A person becomes righteous, by having all sin removed.)
Then he suffered him.
(That is why Jesus said to John the Baptist:
Thus it becometh us to fulfill all righteousness.
Buried means completely under the water.)

And Jesus, when he was baptized,
went up straightway out of the water: (which means that he was totally in the water)
and,
lo, the heavens were opened unto him,
and he saw the Spirit of God descending like a dove,
and lighting upon him:
and lo a voice from heaven,
saying,
"this is my beloved Son, in whom I am well pleased".

Note:
That is what God says to everyone, when they get baptized.
This business of being freed from sin,
by having the body of sin destroyed in water baptism
is not easily believed by everyone.
That is why Jesus said to John the Baptist:
"to fulfil all righteousness."
When we put on Christ, we are joined.
Christ's spirit lives in us and our spirit is in Christ Jesus.

God explains it clearly:
Romans 8:1-2
There is therefore now no condemnation
to them which are in Christ Jesus,
who walk not after the flesh, but after the Spirit.
For the law of the Spirit of life in Christ Jesus
hath made me free from the law of sin and death.

Note:
So when we get buried in baptism,
we put on Christ, and we are no longer two,
but one. We don't put on Christ physically.
Rather, we put on the Spirit of Christ.
This all happens when we are baptized "into Jesus Christ".

Romans 8:8-9
So then they that are in the flesh cannot please God.
But ye are not in the flesh, but in the Spirit
if so be that the Spirit of God dwell in you.
Now if any man have not the "Spirit of Christ",
he is none of his.

(Wow, if we have not put on the spirit of Christ, we are none of his !)

When we are buried with him by baptism into death and then rise and put on the Spirit of Christ, and have fellowship with him, then his blood cleanseth us from all sin.
1 John 1: 6-7 If we say that we have fellowship with him, and walk in darkness, we lie, and do not the truth:
But if we walk in the light , as he is in the light, we have fellowship one with another,
and the blood of Jesus Christ his Son cleanseth us from all sin.
1 John 1

Question: what happens with fornication when we have "put on Christ"?

1 Corinthians 6: 15-19

Know ye not that your bodies are the members of Christ?
shall I then take the members of Christ,
and make them the members of an harlot?
God forbid.
What ? know ye not that he which is joined to an harlot is one body?
For two saith he, shall be one flesh.
But he that is joined unto the Lord is one spirit.
Flee fornication.
Every sin that a man doeth is without the body;
But he that committeth fornication sinneth against his own body.
What? know ye not that your body is the temple of the Holy Ghost
which is in you, which ye have of God, and ye are not your own?
For ye are bought with a price:
therefore glorify God in your body,
and in your spirit, which are God's.

Note:

I believe that the urgency to water baptize also has great influence
in resisting the devil. Satan is not afraid of Humans,
but when we have "put on Christ" we have the strongest defence.
After a person goes through the repentance before God,
and says a sinner's prayer,
believing that Christ Jesus came in the flesh from God,
and shed his blood for us,
and confessing out loud that King Jesus is his Lord
who took our punishment upon himself on the Cross,
this person needs to "put on the spirit of Christ".

Galatians 3:27

God has said,
"For as many as have been baptized "into Christ",
have put on Christ.

Note:
When Christ lives in you, (you have put on Christ, actually the Spirit of Christ)
you have the ability to stand against the wiles of the devil.

Question: does this water baptism, being buried with Christ to have our sins removed,
have any consequence into the "entire worldwide body of Christ",
being accepted into Christ's "worldwide church"?

God says in: ***1 Corinthians 12:12-14***

For as the body is one,
and hath many members,
and all the members of that one body,
being many,
are one body:
so also is Christ.
For by one Spirit are we all "baptized into one body",
whether we be Jews or Gentiles,
whether we be bond or free;
and have been all made to drink into one Spirit.
For the body is not one member,
but many.

Note:
How do we join the worldwide body of Christ ?
It says: for by one Spirit are we all "baptized into one body".
Question: So what actually happens,
when a person gets buried in water baptism?

God says in: ***Galatians 2:20***

I am crucified with Christ (Romans 6:3)
nevertheless I live;
yet not I,
but Christ liveth in me:

and the life which I now live in the flesh
I live by the faith of the Son of God,
who loved me ,
and gave himself for me

When we get water baptized in "the name of the Lord Jesus",
Christ then lives in us.

Question: The men in the Bible, always teach water baptism,
right after leading someone to the Lord.

The Acts 22:14-16
And he said,
the God of our fathers hath chosen thee,
that thou shouldest know his will,
and see that Just One,
and shouldest hear the voice of his mouth.
For thou shalt be his witness unto all men
of what thou hast seen and heard.
And now
why tarriest thou?
Arise, and be baptized,
and wash away thy sins, (baptizing washes away your sins)
calling on the name of the Lord.

The Acts 16:30-34
And he brought them out,
and said,
Sirs,
what must I do to be saved?
And they said,
believe on the Lord Jesus Christ,
and thou shalt be saved, and thy house.
And they spake unto him the word of the Lord,
and to all that were in his house. (There should always be teaching before baptizing)
And he took them the same hour of the night,

and washed their stripes;
and was baptized,
he and all his,
straightway.

The Acts 10:44-48
While Peter yet spake these words,
the Holy Ghost fell on all them which heard the word.
And they of the circumcision which believed (Jews that had become Christians)
were astonished,
because that on gentiles also
was poured out the gift of the Holy Ghost.
For they heard them speak with tongues,
and magnify God.
Then answered Peter,
can any man forbid water,
that these should not be baptized,
which have received the Holy Ghost as well as we?
And he commanded them to be baptized
in "the name of the Lord".

Then prayed they him to tarry certain days.

Question: Is it kind of like a marriage ceremony,
this putting on Christ,
by water baptism?

God says in: ***Ephesians 5:29-32***
For no man ever yet hated his own flesh,
but nourisheth and cherisheth it,
even as the Lord the church:
for we are members of his body,
of his flesh, and of his bones.
For this cause shall a man leave his father and mother ,
and shall be joined unto his wife,
and they two shall be one flesh.
This is a great mystery:
but I speak concerning Christ and the Church.

Note:
Christ and the Church become one flesh.

Ephesians 6:10-12
God has said,
Finally, my brethren,
Be strong in the Lord (now that you have put on Christ)
and in the power of his might.
Put on the whole armour of God,
that ye may be able to stand against the wiles of the devil.
For we wrestle not against flesh and blood,
but against principalities,
against powers,
against the rulers of the darkness of this world,
against spiritual wickedness in high places.

When we have put on the spirit of Christ,
God says in: ***St. John 1:12-13***
But as many as received him, (put on the spirit of Christ)
to them gave he power
to become the sons of God, (we become God's child)
even to them that believe on his name (baptized into the name of Christ Jesus)
which were born, (this is the born again experience)
not of blood,
nor of the will of the flesh,
nor of the will of man,
but of God.
(we surrender our lives to Jesus as our Lord (creator and owner)

Note:
Water baptism in the name of Jesus ,
buried with him by baptism into his death,
to fulfil all righteousness
to be freed from sin,
is the only way to receive the power,

is the only way to put on Christ,
is the only way to be freed from sin,
is the only way to receive the Spirit of Christ
is the only way to then receive
the baptism of the Holy Ghost, by the laying on of hands.

The Acts 2:38 God says :
Then Peter said unto them,
Repent,
And be baptized every one of you
in the name of Jesus Christ
For the remission of sins,
And ye shall receive the gift of the Holy Ghost.

(Jesus is the Comforter, the Holy Ghost)
St. John 16:7
Nevertheless I tell you the truth;
It is expedient for you that I go away,
The Comforter will not come unto you;
But if I depart,
I will send him unto you.

Note:
When Jesus says,
abide in me
and I in you,
that's what he is talking about.

Most pastors have trouble believing that they should be baptizing their people only in the name of the Lord Jesus Christ. It also means that they should be re-baptizing all of their congregation. I have baptized many hundreds of people for the second time,
baptizing them into the name of Christ Jesus, into his death.

The Acts 8:12 But when they believed Philip preaching the things concerning the kingdom of God, and the name of Jesus Christ, they were baptized both men and women.

The Circumcision made without hands
The New Testament Covenant
In the Old Testament God made a contract with Abraham
(Actually the contract was called "a covenant")
If Abraham and his descendants wanted God to be their God,
then they had to accept "Gods Covenant" by circumcision. (***Genesis 17: 7 -14***)

Note:
In our new Covenant with God,
(yes, a Contract for him to be our God)
God has written clearly and warned us
how we should accept his new contract (covenant) :
The Jews all knew that when God referred to their contract (covenant)
they knew it meant the circumcision.
Because without being circumcised, they had no covenant with God.

Colossians 2:8-15
Beware
lest any man spoil you through philosophy and vain deceit,
after the tradition of men,
after the rudiments of the world,
and not after Christ.
For in him dwelleth all the fulness of the Godhead bodily.
And ye are complete in him
which is the head of all principality and power:
in whom ye are "circumcised" with the circumcision made without hands,
in putting off the body of the sins of the flesh
by the circumcision of Christ: (then he explains what
the "Circumcision of Christ" is)
Buried with him in Baptism,
wherein also ye are risen with him
through faith of the operation of God,
who hath raised him from the dead.
And you,

Being dead in your sins and **the uncircumcision of your flesh**,
hath he quickened together with him,
having forgiven you all trespasses;
Blotting out the handwriting of ordinances that was against us, **(Revelation 20:12-13)**
which was contrary to us,
and took it out of the way,
nailing it to his cross;
and having spoiled principalities and powers,
he made a show of them openly,
triumphing over them in it.
Note:
Salvation is only through Jesus Christ.
That is why we are baptised only into "the name Jesus Christ" .
We are baptised into Jesus Christ's death.
When we do that,
God accepts us by covenant because of the "Circumcision of Christ".
We are born again.
And God adopts us by covenant.

Look at where God shows us, that the spirit of God
is the same as the spirit of Christ:

Romans 8:9
But ye are not in the flesh,
but in the Spirit,
if so be that the Spirit of God dwell in you.
Now
if any man have not the Spirit of Christ,
he is none of his.

That definitely precludes, that if we have not been baptized into Christ, and put on Christ, as in Galatians 3:27, we are none of his.
Then we don't belong to God.

Romans 8:14-17
For as many as are led by the Spirit of God,
they are the "sons of God".

For ye have not received the spirit of bondage again to fear;
but
ye have received the Spirit of adoption,
whereby we cry,
Abba,
Father.
The Spirit itself beareth witness with our spirit,
that we are the children of God:
and if children,
then heirs,
heirs of God,
and joint-heirs with Christ;
if so be that we suffer with him, (baptized into Christ's death)
that we may be also glorified together.

CHAPTER 6
Milk 3B - The Baptism of the Holy Spirit

Nicodemus was told that he needed to be
born of water
and of the Spirit
in order to enter into the Kingdom of God. (St. John 3: 3)

First water baptism
and then the baptism of the Holy Spirit.

There are several things that need to be known
about the Holy Spirit.

First :
the baptism of the Holy Spirit
is the only way to receive the power,
to fulfill the last words of King Jesus.

It is not possible to obey King Jesus' last words,
without the baptism of the Holy Spirit.

St. Matthew 16:15-18

And he said unto them,
go ye into all the world,

and preach the gospel to every creature.
He that believeth and is baptized shall be saved;
But he that believeth not shall be damned.
And these signs shall follow them that believe;

1. In my name they shall cast our devils
2. they shall speak with new tongues;
3. they shall take up serpents
4. and if they drink any deadly thing, it shall not hurt them;
5. they shall lay hands on the sick, and they shall recover.

The Acts 1:8

And ye shall receive power,
after that the Holy Ghost is come upon you:
and ye shall be witnesses unto me both in Jerusalem,
and in Samaria,
and unto the uttermost part of the earth.

Second:
Without the baptism of the Holy Spirit,
it is not possible to hear the voice of King Jesus.
God made us to hear his voice.

God says in: ***Deuteronomy 4:36***

> Out of heaven he made thee to hear his voice, (why)
> that he might instruct thee;
> and upon earth he showed thee his great fire;
> and thou heardest his words out of the midst of the fire.

King Jesus also talked about hearing his voice.
God says in: ***St. John 10:27***

> My sheep hear my voice,
> and I know them,
> and they follow me.

King Jesus also made sure
that he wasn't just referring to his immediate disciples,
that would be able to hear his voice.

God says in: ***St. John 10:16***

And other sheep I have ,
which are not of this fold:
them also I must bring,
and they shall hear my voice;
and there shall be one fold,
and one shepherd.

King Jesus also made it very clear,
who can hear his voice.

God says in: ***St. John 8:47***

He that is of God heareth God's words:
Ye therefore hear them not,
because ye are not of God.

Just to be clear, King Jesus also said who "God's sons" really were.

God says in: ***Romans 8:14***

For as many as are led by the Spirit of God,
they are the sons of God.

Christians operate either in the flesh, or in the Holy Spirit.

God says in: ***Romans 8:8***

So then they that are in the flesh cannot please God.

God says in: ***Galatians 6:8***

For he that soweth to his flesh
shall of the flesh reap corruption;
but he that soweth to the Spirit
shall of the Spirit reap life everlasting.

- Obeying the voice of His Majesty King Jesus,
and watching, to see what he wants us to observe,
will result in becoming his servant.

God says in: ***Deuteronomy 28:1***
And it shall come to pass,
if
thou shalt hearken diligently unto
the voice of the Lord thy God,

1. to observe
2. and to do

all his commandments
which I command thee this day,
that the Lord thy God will set thee on high
above all nations of the earth:

Note:
It's an obedience factor.
He will be instructing. (That he might instruct thee)
It's to observe - watch what he is showing us right now
And also to do - he is showing us something to do
- there will be some sort of action involved

Third:

Question: How do people get the baptism of the Holy Spirit?

God says in: ***The Acts 8:14-17***

> Now when the apostles which were at Jerusalem
> heard that Samaria had received the word of God,
> they sent unto them Peter and John:
> who,
> when they were come down,
> prayed for them,
> that they might receive the Holy Ghost.
> (For as yet he was fallen upon none of them:
> only they were baptized in "the name of the Lord Jesus".)
> Then they laid hands on them,
> and they received the Holy Ghost.

Question: Did St. Paul also lay hands on people
to receive the Holy Ghost?

God says in: ***The Acts 19:1-6***

And it came to pass,
that ,
while Apollos was at Corinth,
Paul having passed through the upper coasts came to Ephesus:
and finding certain disciples,
He said unto them,
Have ye received the Holy Ghost since ye believed?
and they said unto him,
We have not so much as heard
whether there be any Holy Ghost.
And he said unto them,
Unto what then were ye baptized?
And they said, unto John's baptism.

Then said Paul,
John verily baptized with the baptism of repentance,
saying unto the people,
that they should believe on him which should come after him,
that is, on Christ Jesus.
When they heard this,

they were baptized
in the name of the Lord Jesus. (they were baptized again)
Note:
They were not baptized into the name of the Father,
because the Father never died,
nor into the name of the Holy Ghost,
because the Holy Ghost never died either.
We only get baptized into Christ's death.)

> And when Paul had laid his hands upon them,
> the Holy Ghost came on them;
> and they spake with tongues,
> and prophesied.

Note:
All the really good stuff that God has for his children,
here on Planet Earth,
is contingent
upon receiving the "baptism of the Holy Spirit".
Without the baptism of the Holy Spirit,
there is no power to perform the gifts of the Holy Spirit.

The 9 Gifts of the Holy Spirit

Note:
This whole Chapter is about the gifts of the Holy Spirit,
and the operation of the Holy Spirit

1 Corinthians 12:1-12
Now
concerning spiritual gifts, (they are not something that you can earn,
they are gifts) brethren,
I would not have you ignorant.

Ye know that ye were Gentiles
carried away unto these dumb idols,
even as ye were led.
Wherefore I give you to understand,
that no man speaking by the "Spirit of God"
calleth Jesus accursed:
and that no man can say "that Jesus is the Lord",
but by the Holy Ghost.
(In other words, you cannot make him your Lord, your master,
unless you are able to hear his voice. As master
he will instruct you.
You will be his servant. And you cannot hear his voice
unless you have the baptism of the Holy Spirit.)

Now
there are diversities of gifts,
but the same Spirit.
And
there are differences of administrations
but the same Lord.
And there are diversities of operations,
But
it is the same God which worketh all in all.
But
the manifestation of the Spirit is given to every man to profit withal.

The Nine Gifts

For to one is given by the Spirit

1. the word of wisdom;

to another

2. the word of knowledge by the same Spirit;

to another

3. faith by the same Spirit;

to another

4. the gifts of healing by the same Spirit;

to another

5. the working of miracles;

to another

6. prophecy

to another

7. discerning of spirits;

to another

8. divers kinds of tongues;

to another

9. the interpretation of tongues:

but
all these worketh that one and the selfsame Spirit,
dividing to every man
severally
as he will.

For
as the body is one,
and hath many members,
and all the members of that one body,
being many,
are one body:
so also is Christ.

Note:
It is important for the five fold ministries
to sort out who has which gifts,
in a church.
These gifts should be experimented and determined,
if they are valid.
If they are real,
then that person should know that God will never take back that gift
that they have received.

Romans 11:29

For the gifts and calling of God
Are without repentance.

Note:
Many Churches refuse to accept the Baptism of the Holy Spirit,
with the resulting tongues and interpretation of tongues and prophesy.

Having the baptism of the Holy Spirit is useless
unless it is operational.
Around 1978 to 1985 Joel Chapter 2, and Acts Chapter 2 happened.

Joel 2: 28-29
And it will come to pass afterward,
that I will pour out my spirit upon all flesh;
and your sons and your daughters shall prophesy,
and your old men shall dream dreams,
your young men shall see visions:
And also upon the servants and upon the handmaids
in those days will I pour out my spirit.
It is very important to note:
that unless people are in servant mode, they shouldn't expect to receive
the "Baptism of the Holy Spirit."
It's the "Abiding in the vine thing" of St. John 15.
That's why it says in Joel: "upon the servants"
will I pour out my Spirit.

The Acts 2: 17 -18

And it shall come to pass in the last days, saith God,
I will pour out of my spirit upon all flesh:
and your sons and your daughters shall prophesy,
and your young men shall see visions,
and your old men shall dream dreams:
and on my servants and on my handmaids I will pour out in those days my spirit;
and they shall prophesy.

Note:

During those years (1978 to 1985) many Christian groups had a drive on for the baptism of the Holy Spirit.
Most people who got baptized, never got to use their gifts.
They would go back to their churches, and nothing would happen.
Primarily because no one was teaching that their was more.
And most pastors were full of fear that this whole thing would go wrong.
They didn't know that it does not hinge on human skill.
Pastors would actually prefer that their board of directors
and some of their elders would get these gifts and no one else.
That way they might control it all.
But God chooses the weak to confound the wise.
That's where it gets confusing.
Even today, you would be hard pressed to find anyone
that knows how to get a church operational in the gifts.
It always hurts me, especially in Pentecostal churches,
where they sing and then sing in the spirit in tongues,
and then the song leader quickly goes on to the next song,
before anything can happen.
In the nine gifts, the fourth one is listed as Gifts of healing. So there are more than one gift type , of healings. I know of a man who mostly is involved with leg bone and foot bone healings.
I know of another man who is mostly involved with opening blind eyes and deaf ears.
I knew a lady who was mostly involved with stomach issues.

Worshipping God in the spirit

Speaking in tongues is totally ignored in most churches.
In most churches it is actually forbidden.
Singing in tongues
and praying in tongues is very rare.
But
King Jesus told us about worshipping God in the spirit.
It's not even optional.

St. John 4:23-24

But the hour cometh
and now is,
when the true worshippers
shall worship the Father
in spirit
and in truth:
for the father seeketh such to worship him.

God is a spirit:
and they that worship him,
must worship him
in spirit and in truth.

That word "must" makes it not optional.

The Bible is not a "book of suggestions".

CHAPTER 7
Milk 4. - The laying on of Hands

Laying on of hands, started in the Old Testament.
There is a transfer of power from your hands to whomever you lay your hands on.
There is also a transfer of power when someone else lays their hands on you.

1 Timothy 5:22
Lay hands suddenly on no man,
neither be a partaker of other men's sins:
keep thyself pure.
Note:
It's not a joke.
Beware.
Study what the Holy Bible actually says.

Leviticus 4:3-4 (also ***Leviticus 4:22-24, 4:27-29, and 4:32-33.)***
If the priest that is anointed do sin
according to the sin of the people;
then let him bring for his sin,
which he hath sinned,
a young bullock without blemish
unto the Lord for a sin offering.
And he shall bring the young bullock
unto the door of the tabernacle of the congregation,
before the Lord;

and shall lay his hand upon the bullock's head,
and kill the bullock before the Lord.

Note:
In doing so
the sin of the priest was transferred to the bullock
and the bullock now full of sin
needed to be immediately killed,
so that no one else would receive those sins.
Even in Romans chapter 6
it says that "he that is dead is freed from sin".

- It always bothers me
  when every older adult
  always wants to touch the head of young children and babies.

You have probably concluded,
that it is also not a great idea
to shake hands with everyone,
or to hug just anyone,
and pat them on the back.

Leviticus 16:21-22
And Aaron shall lay both his hands upon the head of the live goat,
and confess over him all the iniquities of the children of Israel,
and all their transgressions in all their sins,
putting them upon the head of the goat,
and shall send him away by the hand of a fit man into the wilderness:
and the goat shall bear upon him all their iniquities unto a land not inhabited:
and he shall let go the goat in the wilderness.
Note:
This transfer of sins can also be done to a human being.

Leviticus 24:11-16
And the Israelitish woman's son
"blasphemed the name of the Lord"
and "cursed".

And they brought him unto Moses:
(and his mother's name was Shelomith,
the daughter of Dibri, of the tribe of Dan)
And they put him in a ward,
that the mind of the Lord
might be showed them.
And the Lord spake unto Moses,
saying,
bring forth him that hath cursed without the camp;
and let all that heard him,
lay their hands upon his head,
and let all the congregation stone him.
And thou shalt speak unto the children of Israel,
saying,
whosoever curseth his God shall bear his sin.
And he that blasphemeth the name of the Lord,
he shall surely be put to death,
and all the congregation shall certainly stone him:
as well the stranger,
as he that is born in the land,
when he blasphemeth the name of the Lord,
shall be put to death.

Note:
Nothing has changed.
Only the punishment is delayed
until the books will be opened in heaven. ***(Revelation 20:12)***

Exodus 20:7 is still the commandment that has a guilty stamp.
Taking the name of the Lord our God in vain, is still a guilty command.
Any swear word that starts out "Holy ----------" is sin.
Holy, is our God.
If you say "Holy crap" you are saying that God who is Holy is crap.

King Jesus was full of the Holy Spirit.
So when someone touched him,
a transfer of power was released.
If Jesus touched anyone, a transfer of power was also released.
St. Matthew 9:18-26

While he spake these things unto them,
behold there came a certain ruler, and worshipped him,
saying,
my daughter is even now dead:
but come and lay thy hand upon her,
and she shall live.
And Jesus arose,
and followed him,
and so did his disciples.

And behold,
a woman which was diseased with an issue of blood twelve years,
came behind him,
and touched the hem of his garment:
for she said within herself,
if I may but touch his garment
I shall be whole.
But
Jesus turned him about,
and when he saw her,
he said,
daughter be of good comfort;
thy faith hath made thee whole.
And the woman was made whole from that hour.

And when Jesus came into the ruler's house,
and saw the minstrels and the people making a noise,
He said unto them,
give place:
for the maid is not dead,

but sleepeth.
And they laughed him to scorn.
But
when the people were put forth,
he went in ,
and took her by the hand,
and the maid arose.
And the fame hereof went abroad into all that land.

When Jesus touched the girls hand, the power was released.
St. Matthew 9:27-30

And when Jesus departed thence,
two blind men followed him,
crying,
and saying,
thou son of David,
have mercy on us.
And when he was come into the house,
the blind men came to him:
and Jesus saith unto them,
believe ye that I am able to do this?
They said unto him,
yea Lord.

Then he touched their eyes,
saying according to your faith be it unto you.
And their eyes were opened;
and Jesus straitly charged them,
saying,
see that no man know it.
But they ,
when they were departed,
spread abroad his fame in all that country.

CHAPTER 8
Milk 5 : The resurrection of the dead

Our next generation, will likely experience 666
A beast will rise up out of the sea.

Very soon ,
somewhere on planet earth
a beast will rise up out of the sea,
having seven heads and ten horns
and he looks like a leopard.

Revelation 13:1-2
And I stood upon the sand of the sea,
and saw a beast rise up out of the sea,
having seven heads and ten horns, and upon his horns ten crowns,
and upon his heads the "name of blasphemy"
And the beast which I saw was like unto a leopard,
and his feet were as the feet of a bear,
and his mouth as the mouth of a lion:
and the dragon gave him his power,
and his seat,
and great authority.

Revelation 13: 8
And all that dwell upon the earth shall worship him,
whose names are not written
in the "Book of Life" of the Lamb slain
from the foundation of the world.

Revelation 13:13
And he doeth great wonders,
so that he maketh fire come down from heaven
on the earth in the sight of men.
Revelation 13:16-18
And he causeth all,
both small and great,
rich and poor,
free and bond,
to receive a mark in their right hand,
or in their foreheads:
and that no man might buy or sell,
save he that had the mark,
or the name of the beast,
or the number of his name.
here is wisdom.
Let him that hath understanding count the number of the beast:
for it is the number of a man:
and his number is 666.

Revelation 20:4-6 The First Resurrection !
And I saw thrones,
and they sat upon them,
and judgment was given unto them:
and I saw the souls of them "***that were beheaded***"
for the witness of Jesus,
and for the word of God,
and which had not worshipped the beast,
neither his image,
neither had received his mark upon their foreheads,
or in their hands:
and they lived with Christ a thousand years.
But
the rest of the dead lived not again
until the thousand years were finished.

This is the ***first resurrection***. (It says this, right here in Revelation 20
The people in the first one were beheaded)
Blessed and Holy is he
that hath part in the "***first resurrection***"***:***

On such the second death hath no power,
But they shall be priests of God and of Christ,
and shall reign with him a thousand years.

Note:
It will make very good sense to take the mark.
There will be no more theft.
Almost no crime.

The beasts computer will control
all your money,
all your income,
all your payments,
and all your taxes.
And if you don't accept the mark,
you will be an enemy of the state, and get your head cut off.

It only takes one second to get your head cut off.
However this is still very much better
than spending all eternity in the lake of fire.

The question is:
what will you be doing now ,
to inform

all your siblings,
all your children,
all your friends,
all the people you work with,
all your neighbours,
everyone you know,
not to take the mark.

This is extremely serious.
Once the beast is here it will be too late.

People everywhere
need to secure their relationship with the Lord.
That relationship needs to be tight,
as preparation
for the times just ahead of us
regarding 666.

Salvation is still our main thrust.
but
we are in a different era
than all previous generations.
We are on the brink of a terrible period for all Christians.

And
the Bible says many will be deceived.
We will be
tortured,
ridiculed,
named enemies of the state,
turned in by our own families,
and eventually have our heads cut off,
because
we cannot submit to 666,
and the worship of the beast.
It will be similar
to when the Christians in Rome
were led to the colosseum
to be eaten by the lions.

The antichrists are already here.
God says in: ***1 John 2:18-20***
Little children,
it is the last time:
and as ye have heard

that antichrist shall come,
even now there are many antichrists:
whereby we know
that it is the last time.
They went out from us,
But they were not of us;
for if they had been of us,
the would no doubt have continued with us:
but
they went out,
that they might be made manifest
that they were not all of us.
But
ye have an unction from the Holy one,
and ye know all things.

Note:
How soon will the first beast rise up out of the sea?
How soon will the second beast come up out of the earth?

Do you think the money systems are failing?
Do you think the stage is set for the mark system?
Do you think there is anything more important
than getting this message out to everyone?

God says in: ***Revelation 14:9-11***
And the third angel followed them,
saying with a loud voice,
"if any man worship the beast and his image,
and receive his mark in his forehead,
or his hand,
the same shall drink of the wine of the wrath of God,
which is poured out without mixture
into the cup of his indignation;
and he shall be tormented with fire and brimstone
in the presence of the Holy Angels,

and in the presence of the Lamb:
and the smoke of their torment ascendeth up for ever and ever:
and they have no rest day and night,
who worship the beast and his image,
and whosoever receiveth his mark of his name.

Note:
It's going to be extremely hard
for Christians to resist taking the number 666,
because
it will make so much sense to take it.
Since you can only buy or sell with this number,
it will be very difficult to be corrupt.
The mainframe computers will keep track of every transaction.
No one will steal.
It will automatically deduct
your pensions,
your medical,
your debt payments
your mortgage,
and your income taxes.
It will track your education,
your job history,
your medical history
and your insurance history.
The mark will also be a GPS under your skin,
so that computers can follow you everywhere.

The entire DNA identification system,
that everyone is so keen to co-operate with now,
is just a preliminary to 666.
People are thinking that it is an Ancestry system.
But it is actually to identify you and all of your clan.
Christians will be identified as enemies of the State.

They will justify torturing Christians

to make you submit to the mark,
because crime will almost be eliminated in this new order.

Peace and safety.
Christians will be the new terrorists.
The beast will be presented as the new ruler of peace.
There will be no actual money.
Only digital currency.
There will be no counterfeit money.
There will be no laundering.
All deductions will be made automatically.
It will make sense to everyone.
And Christians who don't submit to 666
and refuse the mark,
will be first tortured,
and then they will have their heads cut off.

It will be published ,
what a disgrace Christians were to this perfect society.
It will be horrible for Christians.
But
the alternative is even worse.
The reward in heaven is worth it .

St. Mark 13:8-13
For nation shall rise up against nation,
and kingdom against kingdom:
and there shall be earthquakes in divers places (several places)
and there shall be famines and troubles:
these are the beginning of sorrows.

But
take heed to yourselves:
for they shall deliver you up to councils;
and in the synagogues ye shall be beaten:
and ye shall be brought before rulers and kings for my sake,
for a testimony against them.

And the gospel must first be published among all nations.
But
when they shall lead you,
and deliver you up,
take no thought beforehand what ye shall speak,
neither do ye premeditate:

but
whatsoever shall be given you in that hour,
that speak ye:
for it is not ye that speak,
but the Holy Ghost.

Now
the brother shall betray the brother to death,
and the father the son;
and children shall rise up against their parents,
and shall cause them to be put to death.

And ye shall be hated of all men for my name's sake:
and he that shall endure unto the end,
the same shall be saved.

Don't you wish that none of this were true.

Most people say
that we will all be lifted out of here with the rapture,
before all the bad stuff starts.
Satan loves that,
because
then those people
won't be prepared for the time of 666.
Those non prepared Christians won't realize
the detriment of accepting "the mark of the beast".
And as soon as they receive the mark,
they have lost their access to heaven.
They have chosen the wrong side.

It is a matter of making the right choice.
It's a choice between spending all those trillions times trillions of years burning in the lake of fire;
or living in "perfect heaven" forever.

The resurrection of the dead

People are hoping
that the Christians are leaving first,
and after the rapture,
the unsaved will suffer through all the fire turmoil.

A false prophet named John Nelson Darby
began a theory between December 1826 and January 1827
about Jesus coming back to gather his saints
before the tribulation things would start.
He published his Rapture theory in 1830 and people liked it ,
because it was much more acceptable
than for Christians to have to go through the horrible things
of the end of the world.
The word rapture is not in God's Holy Bible.
C.I Scofield also promoted Darby's Rapture theory.
In the 1970's Hal Lindsey also wrote a book about this rapture theory.
Before 1826 no one had heard of, or mentioned the "Rapture Theology".

King Jesus told us in
St. Matthew 24:21-31

For then shall be great tribulation,
such as was not since the beginning of the world to this time,
no,
nor ever shall be.
And except those days should be shortened,
There should no flesh be saved:
but for the elect's sake
those days shall be shortened.

(***Note:*** Jesus is telling us that the elect will still be here.)

Then, if any man shall say unto you,
Lo, here is Christ, or there;
believe it not.
For there shall arise false Christs,
and false prophets,
and shall show great signs and wonders;
insomuch that ,
if it were possible ,
they shall deceive the very elect. (***The elect have not left yet)***

Behold, I have told you before.
Wherefore
if they shall say unto you,
behold, he is in the desert;
go not forth:
behold he is in the secret chambers;
believe it not.
For as lightning cometh out of the east,
and shineth even unto the west,
so shall also the coming of the Son of man be.
For wheresoever the carcase is,
there will the eagles be gathered together.

Note: Jesus is telling us that after the tribulation in verse 21
He will be coming out of the east.
It seems to me, that King Jesus is not landing anywhere.
Rather, we will meet him in the air and fly away with him.
The reason King Jesus won't land, is that the land below will be desolate.
That is why he says that he won't be in the desert or in secret chambers.

Isaiah 13:9

Behold, the day of the Lord cometh, cruel both with wrath and fierce anger,
to lay the land desolate:
and he shall destroy the sinners thereof out of it.

Note::

There is a false teaching, that Jesus will be landing in the current Jerusalem,
as the returning King, to start his kingdom here on earth.
After the tribulation,
King Jesus will return in the air,
to gather is saints in the air.
The Christians who have died
before Jesus comes back
will be rising to meet King Jesus in the air
on the last day of Planet Earth,
and then the Christians who are alive and remain,
shall be joining them in the clouds,
and then we will all meet King Jesus in the air,
and so shall we ever be with the Lord.

1 Thessalonians 4:16-17

For the Lord himself shall descend from heaven
with a shout,
with the voice of the archangel,
and with the trump of God:
and the dead in Christ shall rise first:
then
we which are alive and remain
shall be caught up together with them in the clouds,
to meet the Lord in the air:
and so shall we ever be with the Lord.

Note:

Apparently, all of this will happen very quickly.
As quickly as a person can blink.

1 Corinthians 15:51-52

Behold,
I show you a mystery;
we shall not all sleep,
but

we shall all be changed,
in a moment,
in the twinkling of an eye,
at the last trump:
for the trumpet shall sound,
and the dead shall be raised incorruptible,
and we shall be changed.

Note:

There will still be people that don't want to believe,
that we will be going through all of the trouble in the tribulation.
Why didn't King Jesus correct Martha
when he was about to raise Lazarus from the dead.
Why didn't he tell Martha that the Christians would be out of here
before the last day?

St. John 11:21-24

Then said Martha unto Jesus,
Lord, if thou hadst been here, my brother had not died.
But I know, that even now,
what soever thou wilt ask of God,
God will give thee.
Jesus said unto her ,
thy brother shall rise again.
Martha saith unto him,
I know that he shall rise again in the resurrection at the last day.

Note:

King Jesus did not correct her.
The resurrection is the last day.

CHAPTER 9
Milk 6 - Eternal Judgement

Eschatology : The part of "Theology" concerned with
* Death,
* Judgment,
* and the final destiny of the soul.

Salvation through fire
This is what coming to the light is all about.

Among Christians, there are many versions of "salvation".
The most common version is the basics of

St. John 3:16-17

For God
so loved the world,
that he gave his only begotten Son,
that whosoever believeth in him
should not perish,
but
have everlasting life.
For God sent not his Son into the world to condemn the world;
but that the world through him might be saved.

Note:
And most Christians went to a meeting and accepted this thought,

and went home relieved, that they had changed sides.
However, in most cases, they never get to hear the rest of the story.
It's right there, in the next four verses.

St. John 3:18-22
He that believeth on him is not condemned:
But he that believeth not
Is condemned already,
because
he hath not believed in the name (it's all about the name Jesus)
of the only begotten Son of God.

(So, what is this condemnation?)

And this is the condemnation,
that light is come into the world,
and men loved darkness rather than light, (why?)
because their deeds were evil.
For every one that doeth evil,
hateth the light,
neither cometh to the light,
lest his deeds should be reproved.
But
he that doeth truth
Cometh to the light,
that his deeds may be made manifest,
that they are wrought in God.

Note:
This whole talk by King Jesus is about how "this salvation works out".
And also "how it works out for them that won't have salvation".
Salvation includes "doing truth". (Why?)
Because then you are "able to come to the light".
And those that continue doing evil "cannot come to the light".
If this conversation by King Jesus is all about salvation,
why did he include this part?
Because that is how it is going to end up.

Right after teaching about salvation,
Jesus and his disciples went into the land of Judea,
and they baptized people.
Jesus was explaining to the ruler of the Jews, that Pharisee named Nicodemus, the reason and the result of being born again, or what happens if you are not born again.

These next verses are about coming to the light.

2 Thessalonians 2:8
And then shall that wicked be revealed,
whom the Lord shall consume
with the spirit of his mouth,
and shall destroy
with the brightness of his coming.

Note:
When King Jesus comes back
will this fire consuming before him
actually be the judgment of the wicked?

1 Corinthians 3:13-15
Every mans work shall be made manifest
for the day shall declare it,
because it shall be revealed by fire;
and the fire shall try every man's work
of what sort it is.

If any man's work abide there upon,
he shall receive a reward.
If any man's work shall be burned,
He shall suffer loss:
but he himself shall be saved
yet so by fire.

2 Thessalonians 1:7-10
And you who are troubled, rest with us,
when the Lord Jesus shall be revealed from heaven

with his mighty angels,
in flaming fire, (This is the light that Jesus was talking about, "coming to the light".

This is what happens to the unsaved)
taking vengeance on them that know not God,
and obey not the Gospel of our Lord Jesus Christ:
who shall be punished with everlasting destruction
from the presence of the Lord,
and from the glory of his power;
(and this is what happens to the saved people)
when he shall come to be glorified in his saints,
and to be admired in all them that believe
(because our testimony among you was believed
in that day.)

Psalms 50:3-6
Our God shall come,
and shall not keep silence:
a fire shall devour before him,
and it shall be very tempestuous round about him.
He shall call to the heavens from above,
and to the earth,
that he may judge his people.
Gather my saints together unto me;
those that have made a covenant (water baptism)
by sacrifice (Jesus is that sacrifice)
And the heavens shall declare his righteousness:
for God is judge himself. Selah.

Zephaniah 3:8-9
Therefore
wait ye upon me,
saith the Lord,
until that day that I rise up to the prey:
for my determination is
to gather the nations,

that I may assemble the kingdoms,
to pour upon them mine indignation,
even all my fierce anger:
for all the earth shall be devoured
with the fire of my jealousy.
For then will I return to the people a pure language,
that they may all call upon the name of the Lord,
to serve him with one consent.

Ezekiel 22:19-22

Therefore, thus saith the Lord God:
because ye are all become dross,
behold,
therefore I will gather you into the midst of Jerusalem,
as they gather silver,
and brass,
and iron,
and tin,
into the midst of the furnace,
to blow fire upon it,
to melt it;
so will I gather you in mine anger
and in mine fury,
and I will leave you there,
and melt you.
Yea,
I will gather you,
and blow upon you in the fire of my wrath,
and ye shall be melted in the midst thereof;
as silver is melted in the midst of the furnace,
so shall ye be melted
in the midst thereof;
and ye shall know that I the Lord
have poured out my fury upon you.

Isaiah 13:6-11

Howl ye:
for the day of the lord is at hand;
it shall come as a destruction from the Almighty
Therefore shall all hands be faint,
and every man's heart shall melt:
and they shall be afraid:
pangs and sorrows shall take hold of them;
they shall be in pain
as a woman that travaileth:
they shall be amazed one at another;
their faces shall be as flames.
Behold
the day of the lord cometh,
cruel
both with wrath and fierce anger
to lay the land desolate:
and he shall destroy the sinners thereof out of it.
For the stars of heaven
and the constellations thereof
shall not give their light:
the sun shall be darkened in his going forth,
and the moon shall not cause her light to shine.
And I will punish the world for their evil,
and the wicked for their iniquity;
and I will cause the arrogancy of the proud to cease,

The heavens being on fire shall be dissolved, against the day of judgment

2 Peter 3:11-14
Seeing then
that all these things shall be dissolved,
what manner of persons ought ye to be
in all holy conversation
and godliness.
Looking for
and hasting unto
the coming of the day of God,
wherein
the heavens being on fire shall be dissolved,
and the elements
shall melt with fervent heat?
Nevertheless we,
according to his promise,
look for new heavens
and for a new earth,
wherein dwelleth righteousness.
Wherefore ,
beloved,
seeing that ye look for such things,
be diligent
that ye may be found of him in peace
without spot,
and blameless.

2 Peter 3:7-10
But the heavens
and the earth,
which are now,
by the same word
are kept in store,
reserved unto fire
against the day of judgment
and perdition of ungodly men.
But,

beloved,
be not ignorant of this one thing,
that one day is with the Lord
is as a thousand years,
and a thousand years as one day.
The Lord is not slack concerning his promise,
as some men count slackness;
but is longsuffering to us-ward,
not willing that any should perish,
but that all should come to repentance.
But the day of the Lord
will come as a "thief in the night";
in which the heavens shall pass away with great noise,
and the elements shall melt with fervent heat,
the earth also
and the works therein
shall be burned up.
Note:
For 6000 years,
the end (death and heaven and hell)
has always been the same.
Every person that has ever lived
has had to make the choice,
to serve God,
or to believe Satan and go to hell.

It's eternal life in heaven,
or eternal life in the lake of fire.
Not making a choice is still a choice.

Being a good person will not get you salvation.
Salvation is a free gift from God.
The only way to acquire salvation,
is through receiving Jesus Christ as your Lord.

God is recording everything.
Every word we speak.
Everything we do.
It's called our works.
God is recording our works.

St. Matthew 12:36-37
But I say unto you,
That every idle word that men shall speak,
They shall give account thereof in the day of judgment.
For by thy words thou shalt be justified,
and by thy words thou shalt be condemned.

Revelation 20:12
And I saw the dead,
small and great,
stand before God;
and the books were opened,
and another book was opened
which is the book of life:
and the dead were judged out of those things
which were written in the books,
according to their works.

St. Matthew 25:46
And these shall go away into everlasting punishment:
but
the righteous into life eternal.

Note:
God sent his Son 'Christ Jesus", to save us from the punishment of our sins.
All we need to do is :

- Believe in our heart that Jesus came down from heaven to die for our sins.
- Confess with our mouth that God raised him up from the dead.
- Ask God to forgive all your sins.

- Repent of all your sins
- Determine to give your life to the Lord Jesus and serve him.
- Get water baptized in the name of the Lord Jesus
- Get an Elder to lay hands on your head for the gift of the Holy Spirit.
- Get involved with a church to hear the word of God, to build up your faith.
- Tell others about this salvation plan
- Live every day for King Jesus

Hell is in the center of the earth. Under the oceans.
The lake of fire is when all the universe is rolled up as a scroll and forms this enormous lake of fire. Then King Jesus comes back, and this same fire is devouring before him.
And finally the earth melts, and death and hell is thrown into this lake of fire.

Ephesians 4:9
Now that he ascended,
what is it but that he also descended first
into the lower parts of the earth.

St. Matthew 12:40
For as Jonah was three days and three nights in the whale's belly;
so shall the Son of man be three days and three nights
in the heart of the earth.

Numbers 16:31-33
And it came to pass,
as he had made an end of speaking all these words,
that the ground clave asunder that was under them:
and the earth opened her mouth,
and swallowed them up,
and their houses,
and all the men that appertained unto Korah,
and all their goods.
They, and all that appertained to them,

went down alive into the pit,
and the earth closed upon them:
and they perished from among the congregation.

2 Peter 2:4
For if God spared not the angels that sinned,
but cast them down to hell,
and delivered them into chains of darkness,
to be reserved unto judgment.

Revelation 20:12-15
And I saw the dead, small and great,
stand before God;
and the books were opened:
and another book was opened,
which is the book of life:
and the dead were judged out of those things
which were written in the books,
according to their works.
And the sea gave up the dead which were in it;
and death and hell delivered up
the dead which were in them:
and they were judged every man according to their works.
And death and hell were cast into the lake of fire.
This is the second death.
And whosoever was not found written in the book of life
was cast into the lake of fire.

Who is this Judge that adjudicates every mans works?

St. John 5:22
For the Father judgeth no man,
but hath committed all judgment unto the Son.
Note:
It's interesting that our salvation is only through King Jesus,
and in the end,
those that did not accept his free salvation

will be judged by King Jesus.
Not only judged,
but cast into the lake of fire.

Every secret sin that a person has committed is recorded.
The Christian who has confessed his sins to God
no longer has a record of sins.
But the unsaved have it all recorded.

St. Luke 12:2
For there is nothing covered,
that shall not be revealed;
neither hid,
that shall not be known.

Note:
But the saved Christians will not need to stand before King Jesus,
Because they got their reprieve back on planet earth.
King Jesus paid the price for their sins and gave them redemption.

Romans 8:1
There is therefore
now
no condemnation to them which are in Christ Jesus,
who walk not after the flesh,
but after the Spirit.
For the law of the Spirit of life
in Christ Jesus
hath made me free from the law of sin and death.

1 Thessalonians 5:1-9
But of the times and the seasons,
brethren,
ye have no need that I write unto you,
for yourselves know perfectly
that "the day of the Lord"
so cometh

as a thief in the night.
For when they say "peace and safety"
then sudden destruction cometh upon them,
as travail upon a woman with child;
and they shall not escape.
But ye brethren,
are not in darkness,
that
that day should overtake you as a thief.

(We will know the week, but not the day or the hour. St. Matthew 24:36)

Ye are children of light,
and the children of the day:
we are not of the night,
not of darkness.
wherefore let us not sleep,
as do others;
but let us watch and be sober,
For they that sleep,
sleep in the night;
And they that be drunken are drunken in the night.
But let us, who are of the day,
be sober,
putting on the breastplate of faith and love;
and for an helmet, the hope of salvation.
For God hath not appointed us to wrath,
but to obtain salvation
by our Lord Jesus Christ.

St. Matthew 24:29-31

Immediately ***after the tribulation of those days***
shall the sun be darkened,
and the moon shall not give her light,
and the stars shall fall from heaven,
and the powers of the heavens shall be shaken
and then shall appear the sign of the Son of man

in heaven:
and then shall all the tribes of the earth mourn,
and ***they shall see the Son of man coming in the clouds of heaven***
with great power and great glory.
and he shall send his angels with a great sound of a trumpet,
and they shall gather together his elect from the four winds,
from one end of heaven to the other.

Note:
Again, Jesus is teaching us that
after the tribulation,
and after the darkness,
and after the stars fall,
and after the world will be shaken
then his angels will gather his elect.
His majesty, King Jesus,
clearly gave us three examples of who is leaving first
and who will be gathered after the unsaved are burned.

St. Matthew 13:30
Let them both grow together
until the harvest:
and in the time of the harvest
I will say unto the reapers,
gather ye together "first the tares"
and bind them in bundles to burn them:
but gather the wheat into my barn.

St. Matthew 13:37-42
He answered them
and said unto them,
he that soweth the good seed,
is the Son of man;
and the field is the world;
the good seed
are the children of the Kingdom;

but
the tares
are the children of the wicked one
the enemy that sowed them is the devil;
the harvest
is the end of the world
the reapers are the angels.
As therefore the tares are gathered
and burned in the fire
so shall it be in the end of the world.

The Son of man shall send forth his angels,
and they shall gather out of his kingdom
all things that offend
and them which do iniquity.
and shall cast them into a furnace of fire:
there shall be wailing and gnashing of teeth.

St. Matthew 22:10-13
So those servants went out into the highways
and gathered together all
as many as they found,
both bad and good:
and the wedding was furnished with guests.
And when the king came in
to see the guests,
he saw a man
which had not on a wedding garment:
And he said unto him,
friend how camest thou hither
not having a wedding garment?
And he was speechless.
Then said the King to his servants,
bind him hand and foot
and take him away,
and cast him into outer darkness;
there shall be weeping and gnashing of teeth.

St. Matthew 13:47-50

Again,
the kingdom of heaven is like unto a net,
that was cast into the sea,
and gathered of every kind:
which when it was full,
they drew to shore,
and sat down,
and gathered the good into vessels,
but cast the bad away.
So shall it be at the end of the world:
The angels shall come forth ,
and sever the wicked from among the just,
and shall cast them into the furnace of fire:
there shall be wailing and gnashing of teeth.
Jesus saith unto them,
have ye understood all these things?
They say unto him,
yea Lord.

The Question remains: What about the Christians during this fire entry by King Jesus?

1 Thessalonians 5:9-11

For God has "not appointed us to wrath"
but to obtain salvation
by our Lord Jesus Christ
who died for us,
that whether we wake or sleep,
we should live together with him.
wherefore comfort yourselves together,
and edify one another,
even as also ye do.

1 Thessalonians 1:10

And to wait
for his Son from Heaven,
whom he raised from the dead,
even Jesus,
which delivered us
from the wrath to come.

How will King Jesus and his army of angels
know that we are his Christians below?

Ephesians 4:30
And grieve not the Holy Spirit of God,
whereby ***ye are sealed***
unto the day of redemption.

2 Corinthians 1:21-22
Now he which stablisheth us with you in Christ,
and hath anointed us,
is God:
who hath also sealed us
and given us the "earnest of the Spirit" in our hearts.

Ephesians 1:13-14
In whom ye also trusted,
after that ye heard the word of truth,
the gospel of your salvation:
in whom also after that ye believed,
ye were sealed with that Holy Spirit of promise,
which is the "earnest of our inheritance"
until the redemption
of the purchased possession,
unto the praise of his glory.

Revelation 7:1-3
And after these things
I saw four angels
standing on the four corners of the earth,
holding the four winds of the earth
that the wind should not blow on the earth,
or on the sea,
nor on any tree.
And I saw another angel ascending from the east,
having the seal of the living God:
and he cried with a loud voice
to the four angels,
to whom it was given
to hurt the earth
and the sea,
saying
hurt not the earth,
neither the sea,
not the trees,
till we have ***"Sealed the servants" of our God***
in their foreheads.

Note:
This will be a last-minute sealing and saving
of people in Israel ***(Revelation 7:4-14)***
who just became Christians.
They also will need the seal,
so they will not be consumed
with the flaming fire from the mouth of King Jesus.
We have another example of how this seal in our forehead
will protect us during the tribulation period
before King Jesus comes back.

Revelation 8:10
And the third angle sounded,
and there fell a great star from heaven,
burning as it were a lamp,
and it fell upon the third part of the rivers,
and upon the fountains of waters:
and
the name of the star is called "Wormwood":
and the third part of the waters became wormwood:
and many men died of the waters,
because they were made bitter.
And a fourth angel sounded,
and the third part of the sun was smitten,
and the third part of the moon,
and the third part of the stars;
so as the third part of them was darkened,
and the day shone not for a third part of it,
and the night likewise.
And I beheld,
and heard an angel flying
through the midst of heaven,
saying with a loud voice,
woe,
woe,
woe,
to the inhibiters of the earth
by reason of the other voices
of the trumpet of the three angels,
which are yet to sound!

Revelation 9:1-4
And the fifth angel sounded,
and I saw a star fall from heaven unto the earth:
and to him was given the key of the bottomless pit;
And he opened the bottomless pit;
and there arose a smoke out of the pit,

as the smoke of a great furnace;
and the sun and the air were darkened by reason of the smoke of the pit.
and there came out of the smoke
locusts upon the earth:
and unto them was given power,
as the scorpions of the earth have power.

And it was commanded them
that they should not hurt the grass of the earth,
neither any green thing,
neither any tree;
"but only those men
which have not the seal of God in their foreheads".

Note:
We see here how God keeps his promise
that Christians are not appointed unto wrath,
but God will keep his promise
through all the evil things that are ahead of us.

Now look at what these locusts
with the scorpion tails will be doing.

Revelation 9:5-11
And to them it was given that they should not kill them,
but that they should be tormented five months:
and their torment was as the torment of a scorpion
when he striketh a man.
And in those days shall men seek death ,
and shall not find it ;
and shall desire to die,
and death shall flee from them.
And the shapes of the locusts
were like unto horses prepared unto battle;
and on their heads were as it were crowns of gold,
and their faces were as the faces of men.
And they had hair as the hair of women,

and their teeth were as the teeth of lions.
And they had breastplates,
as it were breastplates of iron;
and the sound of their wings
was as the sound of chariots of many horses running to battle.
And they had tails like unto scorpions,
and there were stings in their tails:
and their power was to hurt men five months.
And they had a king over them,
which is
"the angel of the bottomless pit",
whose name in the Hebrew tongue is "Abaddon"
but
in the Greek tongue hath his name "Apollyon".

Genesis 2:1 Thus the heavens and the earth were finished,
and all "the host of them".

Isaiah 47:4 As for our redeemer,
"the Lord of Hosts" is his name, the Holy One of Israel .
(Our God is "Lord of Hosts" over two billion Galaxies)
How will this fire devouring before the Lord Jesus Christ
actually get started ?

Psalms 102: 25-26
Of old thou hast laid the foundations of the earth:
and the heavens are the work of thy hands.
They shall perish,
but thou shalt endure:
yea,
all of them shall wax old like a garment;
as a vesture shalt thou change them,
and they shall be changed.

Hebrews 1:10-12
And thou Lord,
in the beginning

hast laid the foundation of the earth;
and the heavens are the work of thine hands:
They shall perish
but thou remainest;
and they shall wax old as doth a garment;
and as a vesture shalt thou fold them up,
and they shall be changed
but thou art the same,
and thy years shall not fail.

Isaiah 34:4
And all the host of heaven shall be dissolved,
and the heavens shall be rolled together as a scroll:
and all their host shall fall down,
as the leaf falleth off from the vine,
and as a falling fig, from the fig tree.

St. Luke 12:49
King Jesus said:
I am come to send fire on the earth;
and what will I ,
if it be already kindled? (Wow)

Revelation 6:12-17
And I beheld when he had opened the sixth seal,
and, lo,
there was a great earthquake;
and the sun became black as sackcloth of hair,
and the moon became as blood:
And the stars of heaven fell unto the earth,
even as a fig tree casteth her timely figs,
when she is shaken of a mighty wind.
And the heaven departed as a scroll
when it is rolled together ;
and every mountain and island were moved
out of their places.

And the kings of the earth,
and the great men,
and the rich men,
and the chief captains
and every free man,
hid themselves in the dens
and in the rocks of the mountains
and said to the mountains and rocks,
fall on us,
and hide us from the face of him that sitteth on the throne,
and from the wrath of the Lamb:
For the great day of his wrath is come;
and who shall be able to stand?

***Note*:**
People who don't know what is going to happen,
will be full of fear.
They will not be rising in the resurrection.
When the mountains start to fall and melt,
and people everywhere have their faces on fire,
terror will overcome all of these people,
who have not been told what is happening.

Isaiah 24:17-20
Fear
and the pit,
and the snare,
are upon thee,
O inhabitant of the earth.
and it shall come to pass,
that he who fleeth from the noise of the fear ***(fear sends you into the pit)***
shall fall into the pit;
and he that cometh up out of the midst of the pit
shall be taken in the snare:
for the windows from on high are open,

and the foundations of the earth do shake.
The earth is utterly broken down,
the earth is moved exceedingly.
The earth shall reel to and fro like a drunkard,
and shall be removed like a cottage;
and the transgression thereof
shall be heavy upon it;
and it shall fall,
and not rise again.

Note:
Instead,
those that have heard the truth,
and know what is happening
when King Jesus comes back,
will rejoice and be glad.

The legal precedence
that God can spare people
in flaming fire,
is that lovely story in ***Daniel 3: 10-30***
Where Daniel's three friends
Shadrach,
Meshach
and Abednego
never even had the smell of smoke or fire on their clothing,
and suffered no burns in the midst of the hottest furnace.

How does God do that?
We know that God does everything
by speaking it into existence.

Psalms 29:7
The voice of the Lord
divideth the flames of fire.

Hebrews12:29
Our God is a consuming fire.

Note:
Not only will there be fire in the sky
burning people on the ground below,
but the earthquakes will cause the ground to break up
and there will be water like rivers everywhere,
and mountains will be falling.
Does God actually promise
that his people will not be burned in the fire ?
(I actually saw all this in a vision in 1981.
The Lord has given me many visions when I was younger.
Joel 2: 28-29 and Acts 2: 17-18)
Isaiah 43:2
When thou passest through the waters, I will be with thee;
and through the rivers, they shall not overflow thee:
when thou walkest through the fire, thou shalt not be burned;
neither shall the flame kindle upon thee. For I am the Lord thy God.

Isaiah 25:8-9
He will swallow up death in victory;
and the Lord God will wipe away tears
from off all faces;
and the rebuke of his people
shall he take away from off of all the earth
for the Lord hath spoken it.
And it shall be said in that day,
Lo,
this is our God;
we have waited for him,
and he will save us:
this is our Lord;
we have waited for him,
we will be glad
and rejoice in his salvation.

Revelation 21:5-8

And he that sat upon the throne said,
Behold,
I make all things new.
And he said unto me,
Write:
for these words are true and faithful.
And he said unto me,
It is done.
I am alpha and omega,
the beginning and the end.
I will give unto him that is athirst
of the fountain of the water of life freely.

He that overcometh
shall inherit all things;
and I will be his God,
and he shall be my son.
But he fearful,
(this is why we cannot be afraid of the fire and floods)
and the unbelieving,
and the abominable,
and murderers,
and whoremongers,
and sorcerers,
and idolaters,
and all liars,
shall have their part in the lake (this lake is all those galaxies that are rolled up together as a scroll)
which burneth with fire and brimstone:
which is the second death.

CHAPTER 10
Before the "Beginning of Sorrows" begins

Everything is going to change soon.
It's not going to get better.
Christians need to prepare.
That's what this book is about.
"Truth"

St. Luke 21:10-12
Then he said unto them, Nation shall rise against nation,
and kingdom against kingdom:
and great earthquakes shall be in divers places, (the Greek says: from place to place)
and famines, and pestilences;
and fearful sights and great signs shall there be in heaven.
But before all these,
they shall lay their hands on you,
and persecute you,
delivering you up to the synagogues,
and into prisons,
being brought before kings and rulers for my names sake.

Note:
So the first sign,
that the "beginning of sorrows" is starting
will be the persecution of the saints,
with afflictions, (beatings)

with imprisonment,
and some will be put to death.

St. Matthew 24: 3- 9

And as he sat upon the mount of Olives,
the disciples came to him privately,
saying,
tell us when shall these things be?
and what shall be the sign of thy coming,
and of the end of the world?
And Jesus answered and said unto them,
Take heed that no man deceive you. (there will be men that will deceive you)
For many shall come in my name,
saying,
I am Christ;
and shall deceive many.
And ye shall hear of wars and rumours of wars:
see that ye be not troubled:
for all these things must come to pass,
but the end is not yet.
For nation shall rise against nation,
and kingdom against kingdom:
and there shall be
famines,
and pestilences,
and earthquakes, in divers places. (divers means several)
All these are the beginning of sorrows.
Then shall they deliver you up to be afflicted,
and shall kill you:
and ye shall be hated of all nations
for my names sake.

Note:
Unlike all of the generations before us,
We are the
most informed,
most educated,
most read,
most wealthy people ever.

St. Luke 12:48
God says: "to whom much is given,
much is required.

Note:
Therefore
We are going to go through
tests
and trials of our faith,
which are going to be much harder
than generations before us.

Overcoming is rewarded by inheritance

Question: What things are we to overcome?

God says in: **Revelation 21:8**

But the

1. fearful
2. and unbelieving
3. and the abominable
4. and murderers
5. and whoremongers
6. and sorcerers
7. and idolaters
8. and all liars

shall have their part in the lake
which burneth with fire and brimstone:
which is the second death.

Question: If we don't do those things
what is our inheritance like?

God says in: **Revelation 21:7**

He that overcometh shall inherit all things;
and
I will be his God,
and he shall be my son.

Note:
The first thing we need to overcome is fear.
The other side of this coin is trust.
We overcome fear with trust in God.
God controls everything.
We increase our trust by having "fear of the Lord".
Breaking God's laws gets us cut off from his blessings.
This includes not trusting him.
We lose two things:

1. his blessings
2. his protection

Fear of the Lord is part of overcoming!

Every person must decide which side they are on.
The devil's side
or
God's side.
Not deciding is automatically on devil's side.

You can't do a bit of both.
God won't work with you if you cheat on him.
If you are not totally committed to God,
God won't protect you.
Satan's evil brings us nothing but severe trouble.

Question: God calls Satan a thief.
What are Satan's objectives?

God says in: ***St. John 10:10***

The thief cometh not,
but for to steal,
and to kill,
and to destroy:
I am come that they might have life,
and that they might have it more abundantly.

Question: There will always be problem people in our lives,
in which case we then need to make a choice.
What does God suggest?

God says in: ***Proverbs 13:10***

Only by pride cometh contention:
but with the well advised is wisdom.

Question: What would God have us do instead?

God says in: ***Philippians 2:3***

Let nothing be done through strife or vainglory;
But in lowliness of mind
let each esteem the other better than themselves.

Question: How does God expect us to communicate lowliness of mind?

God says in: ***Ephesians 4:29***

Let no corrupt communication proceed out of your mouth,
but
that which is good to the use of edifying, (Lifting up)
that it may minister grace unto the hearers.

God says in: ***2 Timothy 3:1-8***

This know also,
that in the last days
perilous times shall come.
For men shall be lovers of their own selves,
covetous,
boasters,
proud,
blasphemers,
disobedient to parents,
unthankful,
unholy,
without natural affection,
trucebreakers,
false accusers,
incontinent,
fierce,
despisers of those that are good,
traitors,
heady,
high-minded,
lovers of pleasures more than lovers of God,

having the form of godliness,
but denying the power thereof: (***The baptism of the Holy Spirit power***)
from such turn away.

For of this sort are they which creep into houses,
and lead captive silly women laden with sins,
led away with divers lusts, (several lusts)
ever learning,
and never able to come to the knowledge of the truth.

CHAPTER 11
Let us go on unto perfection

Strong Meat

This section about strong meat will help those churches that have by reason of use had their senses exercised.
They are now ready for strong meat.
They are now able to discern both good and evil.

Google says there are about 6.9 billion people in the world.
Google also says there are about 2.18 billion Christians .
Meanwhile, our hospitals are so full of sick people,
that we even have a shortage of nurses and doctors.

King Jesus said that God heals our diseases.

St. Mark 16:16-18
He that believeth and is baptized shall be saved.
But he that believeth not shall be damned.
And these signs shall follow them that believe;
In my name shall they cast out devils;
they shall speak with new tongues;
they shall take up serpents;
and if they drink any deadly thing,
it shall not hurt them;
they shall lay hands on the sick,
and they shall recover.

Note:
So where are these believers?
I have seen many hospital Chaplains,
and I have never seen one who has the gifts of healing.
Why aren't Christians in every hospital
reducing the patient numbers.

Every hospital also has Psychiatric ward,
usually called a Mental Health Ward.
In Jesus' time these people were on the streets.
Now we lock them in wards and feed them pills to subdue them.
Many are demon possessed.
They walk around like zombies. Like the walking dead.

Who is able for Strong meat?

Those that have their senses exercised.
It means that they have become operational
in the gifts of the Holy Spirit,
and can freely function within the spirit realm
to discern good and evil.

This is very rare in most churches.

Strong Meat for Christians
Let us go on unto perfection

Hebrews 5:12-14
For when for the time ye ought to be teachers,
(God expects every new convert to shortly begin
to teach those that the convert has brought to
Christ's salvation, because that is by far the
fastest way to learn. The teacher always learns
the most. And that is one of the first principles
of the oracles of God)
ye have need that one teach you again,

which be the first principles of the oracles of God;
and are become such as have need of milk,
and not of strong meat.

For
everyone that useth milk
is unskillful in the word of righteousness:
for he is a baby.
But
strong meat belongeth to them
that are of full age,
even those who by reason of use
have their senses exercised
to discern both good and evil

Hebrews 6:1-2

Therefore (because of the above statements)
leaving the principles of the doctrine of Christ,
let us go on unto perfection;
not laying again the foundation of

1. repentance from dead works,
2. and of faith toward God,
3. of the doctrine of baptisms, (more than one)
4. and of laying on of hands,
5. and of resurrection of the dead,
6. and of eternal judgment.

CHAPTER 12
The purpose of a Church

The purpose of a church:
should be: that the surrounding neighborhood can go
to hear the kingdom of God preached,
and receive God action for all of their needs.

God says in: ***James 5: 14-15***
Is any sick among you?
Let him call for the elders of the church;
and let them pray over him,
anointing him with oil in the name of the Lord:
and the prayer of faith shall save the sick,
and the Lord shall raise him up;
and if he have committed sins,
they shall be forgiven him.

Note:
Most people that go to church,
don't even know who the elders of that church are.
And most elders don't carry a
"vial of anointing oil" to heal the sick.
Neither do the elders or deacons or pastors or evangelists or prophets or apostles, or teachers or the people with the gift of healing, or the people with the gift of miracles, have name tags with their designation.

Psalms 103:2-3
Bless the lord,
O my soul,
and forget not all his benefits:
who forgiveth all thine iniquities (sins)
who healeth all thy diseases.

St. Matthew 8:16
When the even was come,
they brought unto him many that were possessed with devils:
and he cast out the spirits with his word,
and healed all that were sick.
Note:
Some people say, that was great for Jesus to do that,
but healings were then,
and in our time, we don't have Jesus' power to heal.
But Jesus told us that we can perform healings.

St. John 14:12
Verily,
Verily,
I say unto you,
he that believeth on me,
the works that I do
shall he do also;
and greater works than these shall he do;
because I go unto my Father.
Note:
It is the responsibility of any church
to love their neighbors as themselves.
That includes

1. taking care of the sick
2. taking care of the demon possessed
3. taking care of the poor
4. taking care of the hungry
5. taking care of the messed-up families

6. taking care of the salvation of the neighborhood
7. taking care of the discipleship of the neighborhood
8. taking care of the people
   that have been sent to jail from this neighborhood
9. taking care of the strangers that come into this neighborhood
10. taking care of the orphans and foster kids
    that are in this neighborhood
11. taking care of the widows that are in this neighborhood
12. taking care of those that need clothing

King Jesus trained 12 disciples.
Then king Jesus trained 70 more disciples.

To both groups King Jesus:

- gave them power and authority over all devils
- gave them power to cure diseases
- gave them power to tread on serpents and scorpions
- gave them power over all the enemy
- gave them power over the spirits
- sent them to preach the Kingdom of God
- sent them to heal the sick

And this was King Jesus entire marketing plan to promote
the Kingdom of God. (Salvation)

Apparently, there are 279 million Pentecostal Christians in the world.
Apparently, there are 305 million Charismatic Christians in the world.

Why are they not activated in their communities?

CHAPTER 13
The worship before God's throne

Question: Some churches have kneeling boards,
in front of the benches.
What does God want us to do
when we enter the church to worship?

God says in: ***Psalms 95:6-7***

O Come,
let us worship and bow down:
let us kneel before the Lord our maker.
For he is our God;
and we are the people of his pasture,
and the sheep of his hand.
Today
if ye will hear his voice,
harden not your heart,
as in the provocation,
as in the day of temptation in the wilderness:

Question: How is prayer to be done in churches?

God says in: ***1 Timothy 2:1-3***

I exhort therefore,
that,
first of all,

1. supplications, (kneeling or bending down)
2. prayers,
3. intercessions, (praying for other people)
4. and giving of thanks,

be made for all men;
For Kings,
and for all that are in authority;
that we may lead
a quiet and peaceable life
in all godliness and honesty.
For this is good and acceptable
in the sight of God our Saviour.

Romans 12:1
I beseech you therefore, brethren,
by the mercies of God,
that ye present your bodies a living sacrifice,
holy,
acceptable
unto God
which is your reasonable service.

St. John 4:24
God is a Spirit:
and they that worship him
must worship him
in spirit and in truth.

St Matthew 21:13
And Jesus said unto them,
it is written,
my house shall be called "***the house of prayer";***
but
ye have made it a den of thieves.

1 Timothy 3:15
But
if I tarry long,
that thou mayest know how
thou oughtest to behave thyself
in the house of God,
which is the church of the living God,
the pillar and ground of the truth

Note:
Every Christian church
is meant to be,
the pillar and ground of "the truth".

Of course change can only come if the entire congregation is teachable.
If only a few desire to conform to change, strife will lead to a church split.

There are seven things that God hates"
Proverbs 6:16-19

These six things doth the Lord hate:
yea,
seven are an abomination unto him.

1. A proud look
2. A lying tongue
3. And hands that shed innocent blood
4. An heart that deviseth wicked imaginations,
5. Feet that be swift in running to mischief
6. A false witness that speaketh lies,
7. And he that soweth discord among brethren.

Therefore I have endeavored to circumvent this problem
of "sowing discord among the brethren",
by always presenting theology and doctrine to the top clergy,
rather than to inform and confront individuals from the congregation.

This presentation must always be done with grace,
not accusing anyone,
nor shaming anyone,
but showing that there will always be more to learn.
The more we learn, the more we realize that we are just scratching the surface.
This is true for every faculty of learning.

Religion and tradition are the main source of resistance.
Because someone important has stated the way things should be done,
is not the premise for remaining in the theology of tradition.
The only way change should evolve, and advance,
is by the thorough study of the Holy Bible,
to ensure that it is actually what God meant for us to do.
God's communication to us, must be diligently studied.

God says in: ***Ephesians 6:18***

> Praying always
> with all prayer and supplication in the Spirit (praying in tongues)
> watching thereunto with all perseverance
> and supplication for all saints.

Every knee should bow

Note:
I have been in Hundreds of Churches.
Good Churches.
But
I have never seen a church that bows down at the name of Jesus.
Every time the "Holy name of Jesus" is mentioned anywhere,
the entire church bows down on their knees.
This is the respect for his holiness
and that he has all power in heaven and on earth.
He is the "Supreme Commander" of all those two hundred billion galaxies.

Our galaxy, the Milky way, has about a hundred billion stars.
I have no idea why Churches ignore this command.

Romans 14:11
For it is written,
As I live,
saith the Lord,
every knee shall bow to me,
and every tongue shall confess to God. (Confession is made to God)

It is written:
Philippians 2:9-12
Wherefore God also
hath highly exalted him,
and given him a name above every name:
that
at the name of JESUS
every knee should bow,
of things in heaven,
and things on earth.
and things under the earth;
and
that ***every tongue should confess***
that JESUS CHRIST IS LORD,
to the glory of the Father.

(This is not an optional or casual request by God.)
God goes on to say,
Wherefore , my beloved,
as ye have always obeyed,
not as in my presence only
but now much more in my absence,
work out your own salvation with "fear and trembling".

The Holy Bible is not a book of suggestions.

It is the combination of: "Worshipping God and doing his will"

St. John 9:31
Now we know that God heareth not sinners:
but
if any man be a worshipper of God,
and doeth his will,
him he heareth.

Question: Has God given us instruction, how to "enter his courts, which is his throne room?"

God says in: ***Psalms 100:1-4***
Make a joyful noise unto the Lord, all ye lands.
Serve the Lord with gladness:
Come before his presence with singing.
Know ye not that the Lord he is God:
It is he that hath made us,
and not we ourselves;
we are his people.
and the sheep of his pasture.
Enter into his gates with thanksgiving,
and into his courts with praise:
be thankful unto him,
and bless his name.
For the lord is good:
his mercy is everlasting;
and his truth endureth
to all generations.

Note: "Entering his courts"
God's throne room is not the complaint department.
Nor is it a place to start begging for favours.
He already knows all your needs.

He doesn't require your explanations.
Come with singing
Come with gladness
Come with praise
Come with thanksgiving
Come with blessing of his Holy name.
This is why we always start church with singing.
We are coming into the courts of the Supreme Commander
of all the galaxies in the universe;
right into his throne room.
"Not the place to beg"
When I said it is "not the place to be begging for favours",
you need to understand that God has designed plans
for all of your needs.

If you need money:
Malachi 3:10-11
Bring ye all the tithes into the storehouse,
that there may be meat in mine house,
and prove me now herewith,
saith the Lord of hosts,
if I will not open you the windows of heaven,
and pour you out a blessing,
that there shall not be room enough to receive it.
and,
I will rebuke the devourer for your sakes,
and he shall not destroy the fruits of your ground;
neither shall your vine cast her fruit before the time in the field,
saith the Lord of Hosts.

2 Corinthians 9:6-7
But this I say,
He which soweth sparingly
shall reap also sparingly;
and he which soweth bountifully
shall reap also bountifully.

Every man according as he purposeth in his heart,
so let him give:
not grudgingly,
or of necessity:
for God loveth a cheerful giver.

If you or someone needs a healing
James 5:14

Is any sick among you?
let him call for the elders of the church;
and let them pray over him,
anointing him with oil
in the name of the Lord Jesus
and the prayer of faith shall save the sick,
and the Lord shall raise him up;
and if he have committed sins,
they shall be forgiven him.

If you need a promotion:
Psalms 75:6-7

For promotion cometh neither from the east,
nor from the west
nor from the south,
But God is the judge:
He putteth down one,
and setteth up another.

If you don't know what to do
Proverbs 8:14

Council is mine,
and sound wisdom:
I am understanding;
I have strength.

Proverbs 3:5-7

Trust in the Lord with all thine heart;
and lean not unto thine own understanding.

In all thy ways acknowledge him,
and he shall "direct thy paths".
Be not wise in thine own eyes:
fear the Lord,
and depart from evil.

Question: If we are not very good singers,
does God really want us to make a joyful noise?

God says in: ***Psalms 95:1-2***
O come let us sing unto the Lord:
let us make a joyful noise
to the rock of our salvation.
Let us come before his presence with thanksgiving,
and make a joyful noise unto him with Psalms.

Question: Does God like band music in a church?

God says in: ***Psalms 92:1-3***
It is a good thing to Give thanks unto the Lord,
and to sing praises unto thy name,
O most high:
To show forth thy loving kindness in the morning,
and thy faithfulness every night.
Upon an instrument of ten strings,
and upon the psaltery;
upon the harp with a solemn sound.
Question: How much are we to praise the Lord?

God says in: ***Psalms 113:1-3***
Praise ye the Lord.
Praise ,O ye servants of the Lord,
Praise the name of the Lord.
Blessed be the name of the Lord
from this time forth and for evermore.
From the rising of the sun
unto the going down of the same
the Lord's name is to be praised.

Questions : Does God like us to lift up our hands in church,
when we bless the Lord?

God says in: ***Psalms 134:1-3***

Behold, bless ye the Lord, all ye servants of the Lord,
which by night,
"stand in the house of the Lord".
"Lift up your hands in the sanctuary",
and bless the Lord.
The Lord that made heaven and earth
bless thee out of Zion.

Question: Why does God want us to bless the Lord?

God says in: ***Psalms 103:1-3***

Bless the Lord , O my soul:
and all that is within me, bless his holy name.
Bless the Lord, O my soul,
and forget not all his benefits:
who forgiveth all thine iniquities;
who healeth all thy diseases.

Entering into the worship of God,
is actually coming into his presence.
The presence of God is actually his throne room. Daniel saw it.
Daniel saw other thrones cast down before God . (the thrones of the four beasts)
And then God sat down.

Daniel 7:9–10

I beheld
till the thrones were cast down,
and
the ancient of days did sit,
whose garment was white as snow,
and the hair of his head like the pure wool:
his throne was like the fiery flame,
and his wheels as burning fire.

A fiery stream issued and came forth from before him:
thousand thousands ministered unto him,
and
ten thousand times ten thousand stood before him:
the judgment was set,
and the books were opened.

Note:
John saw it also.
And he wrote it to the churches in Asia.
John saw the seven spirits before the throne of God.

Revelation 1:4
John to the seven churches which are in Asia:
Grace be unto you,
and peace,
from him which is,
and which was,
and which is to come;
and from the seven spirits
which are before his throne.
Note:
John was in the spirit, and he saw God on his throne.

Revelation 4:2–8
And immediately
I was in the spirit:
and ,
behold,
a throne as set in heaven,
and one sat on the throne.
And he that sat was to look upon like a jasper and a sardine stone: (both reddish)
And there was a rainbow round about the throne,

In sight like unto an emerald. (clear green)
And
round about the throne were
four and twenty seats:
and upon the seats I saw four and twenty elders sitting,
clothed in white raiment;
and they had on their heads crowns of gold.
And out of the throne proceeded lightnings and thunderings and voices:
and there were seven lamps of fire burning before the throne,
which are the seven "Spirits of God."
And before the throne there was
a sea of glass like unto crystal:
and in the midst of the throne,
and round about the throne,
were four beasts full of eyes before and behind.
And the first beast was like a lion,
and the second beast like a calf,
and the third beast had a face as a man,
and the fourth beast was like a flying eagle.
And the four beasts had each of them six wings about him;
and they were full of eyes within:
and they rest not day and night,
saying,
Holy,
Holy,
Holy,
Lord God almighty,
which was ,
and is,
and is to come.
And when those beasts give
glory,
and honour,
and thanks to him that sat on the throne
e,

who liveth forever
and ever,
The four and twenty elders fall down before him
that sat on the throne,
and worship him that liveth forever and ever,
and cast their crowns before the throne,
saying,
Thou art worthy,
O Lord,
to receive glory
and honour
and power:
for thou hast created all things,
and for thy pleasure they are and were created.

Note:
This gives us an insight into what is going on at God's throne room.
It give us a new respect
for where we are entering
when we say
"Father God, we come to you in Jesus name".
We are then in the presence of an extremely Holy place.

Giving

Many people stay away from church
because they think that all the church is good for
is demanding them to give money.

1 Chronicles 16:29
Give unto the Lord "the glory due unto his name": (How do we do this?)
Bring an offering,
and come before him:
worship the Lord in the beauty of Holiness.

1 Timothy 6:18-19
That they do good,
that they be rich in good works,
ready to distribute,
willing to communicate;
laying up in store for themselves
a good foundation against the time to come,
That they may lay hold on eternal life.
Malachi 3:8-10
Will a man rob God?
Yet ye have robbed me.
But ye say,
where in have we robbed thee?
In tithes and offerings.
Ye are cursed with a curse:
for ye have robbed me, even this whole nation.
Bring ye all the tithes into the storehouse,
that there may be meat in mine house,
and prove me now herewith, (God sets forth a challenge with a reward)
saith the Lord of hosts,

1. if I will not open you the windows of heaven,
   and pour you out a blessing,
   that there will not be room enough to receive it.
2. And I will rebuke the devourer for your sakes,
   and he shall not destroy the fruits of your ground;
   neither shall your vine cast her fruit before the time in the field,
   saith the Lord of Hosts.

2 Corinthians 9:6-8
But this I say,
he which soweth sparingly
shall reap also sparingly;
and he which soweth bountifully
shall reap also bountifully.
Every man according as he purposeth in his heart,
so let him give;

Not grudgingly,
or of necessity:
for God loveth a cheerful giver.
And God is able to make all grace abound toward you;
that ye always having all sufficiency in all things,
may abound to every good work.

Communion is not an option for Christians

1 Corinthians 11:26-32
For as often as ye eat this bread
and drink this cup,
ye do show the Lord's death till he comes back.
Wherefore
whosoever shall eat this bread,
and drink this cup of the Lord,
unworthily,
shall be guilty of the body and blood of the Lord.
But let a man examine himself,
and so let him eat of that bread,
and drink of that cup.
For he that eateth and drinketh unworthily,
eateth and drinketh damnation to himself,
not discerning the Lord's body.
For this cause many are weak and sickly among you,
and many sleep. (die)
For if we would judge ourselves,
we should not be judged.
But when we are judged,
we are chastened of the Lord,
that we should not be condemned with the world.
Note:
All Churches need to be warning people ,
before they serve the communion.
It is dangerous.

St. John 6:51-58

I am the living bread which came down from heaven:
if any man eat of this bread, he shall live forever:
and the bread that I will give is my flesh,
which I will give for the life of the world.
The Jews therefore strove among themselves,
saying,
how can this man give us his flesh to eat?
Then Jesus said unto them,
Verily
verily,
I say unto you,
except ye eat the flesh of the Son of man,
and drink his blood,
ye have no life in you.
Whoso eateth my flesh,
and drinketh my blood,
hath eternal life;
and I will raise him up at the last day.

For my flesh is meat indeed,
and my blood is drink indeed.
He that eateth my flesh, and drinketh my blood,
dwelleth in me,
and I in him.
As the Father hath sent me,
and I live by the Father :
so he that eateth me,
even he shall live by me.
This is that bread which came down from heaven:
not as your fathers did eat manna
and are dead:
he that eateth of this bread shall live for ever.

Prayer and Worship

Prayer and Worship

Most of the Churches that I have been to
are open for their services once or twice on Sundays.
Some also have Wednesday night prayer
and bible teaching, in the evenings.
The rest of the time the doors are locked.

King Jesus said:
St. Matthew 21:13
And he said unto them,
It is written,
my house shall be called "the house of prayer;"
but
ye have made it a den of thieves.

Note:
Many years ago,
churches,
even on a Sunday morning
would allow people in the congregation
to pray out loud in the audience.
And many would participate,
and it was always very much from the Holy Spirit.
Prayers would not only be said for immediate needs,
but would also be prayed for our people in Government,
our people in authority, like the policemen and judges,
our doctors and nurses,
our people that were sick, and some in the hospital,
our principals and teachers,
our pastors and elders,
and our evangelists and missionaries.
"Parishioners praying" was powerful and necessary.

King Jesus taught us:
St. John 4:23-24
But the hour cometh ,
and now is,
when the true worshippers
shall worship the Father
in spirit and in truth:
for the Father seeketh such to worship him .
God is a Spirit.
and they that worship him
must worship him in spirit and in truth.

King Jesus also taught us:
St. John 17:17
Sanctify them through thy truth:
thy word is truth.

King Jesus also taught us:
St. John 16:13
Howbeit when he,
the Spirit of truth ,
is come,
he will guide you into all truth:
for he shall not speak of himself;
but whatsoever he shall hear,
that shall he speak:
and he will show you things to come.

King Jesus also taught us:
St. John 18:37
Pilate therefore said unto him,
art thou a king then?
Jesus answered ,
thou sayest that I am King.
to this end was I born,
and for this cause came I into the world,

that I should bear witness unto the truth.
Everyone that is of the truth
heareth my voice.

Note:
Almost all of the churches around the world
say that they have the Holy Spirit .
But none of the manifestations of the Holy Spirit
are manifested in most churches.

Words of wisdom are not spoken in their churches.
Words of knowledge are not spoken in their churches.
The Spirit of faith is not evident in their churches.
The gifts of healing are not seen in their churches.
The working of miracles is not seen in their churches.
The gift of prophecy is not heard in their churches.
The discerning of spirits is not seen in their churches.
The speaking of tongues is not heard in their churches.
The interpretation of tongues is not heard in their churches.

CHAPTER 14
The thrust of the church

There are about 29,944 Pastors in the U.S.A.
Today, we really admire the pastors that have huge churches.
The churches with the most people, are the envy of all of the others.
Frequently the ministers of the large churches also have their sermons aired on television, so that millions of people stay at home on a Sunday morning to hear them.
These stay-at-home members, miss out on the fellowship of the saints.
And their children most likely will never enter a church either.

King Jesus taught us:
Hebrews 10:25
Not forsaking the assembling of ourselves together,
as the manner of some is;
but
exhorting one another:
and so much the more,
as ye see the day approaching.

Note:
These large churches have many benefits.
They have a very large budget.
They have the ability to be on television.
They have exceptional buildings.
They have high salaries for the ministerial staff.

All of that is good.
God loves to see huge crowds of people praising him.
But there is more.
We should prepare the congregations,
to mature like King Jesus' disciples did.

King Jesus trained twelve disciples for three years
and then gave them this message:
St. Luke 9: 1-6
Then he called his twelve disciples together ,
and gave them power
and authority
over all devils,
and to cure diseases.
And
he sent them to preach the kingdom of God,
and to heal the sick,
and
he said unto them
take nothing for your journey,
neither staves,
nor scrip,
neither bread,
neither money;
neither have two coats apiece,
And
whatsoever house ye enter into,
there abide,
and thence depart.
And whosoever will not receive you,
when ye go out of that city,
shake off the very dust from your feet
for a testimony against them.
And they departed,
and went through the towns,
preaching the gospel,
and healing every where.

Note:
So, while his twelve disciples were gone,
Jesus trained seventy more disciples,
and got them ready to go out,
just like the first twelve.
It's interesting that King Jesus' objective
wasn't to train them to stay with him,
or to take over some of the local responsibilities.
He trained them to go to people
that needed to turn to God for salvation.
And when they were to go out,
he trained them to heal the sick,
and cast out devils,
so that people were to understand
that God had come to them,
to do God business with them.

In 2023 nothing has changed. This is still God's objective for churches
Luke 10:1-9
After these things
the Lord appointed other seventy also,
and sent them two and two before his face
into very city and place,
whither he himself would come.
Therefore,
said he unto them,
the harvest truly is great ,
but the labourers are few:
pray ye therefore the Lord of the harvest,
that he would send forth labourers into his harvest.
Go your ways:
behold,
I send you forth as lambs among wolves.
Carry neither purse,
nor scrip,
nor shoes:

and salute no man by the way.
And into whatsoever house ye enter,
first say, peace be to this house.
And if the Son of peace be there ,
your peace shall rest upon it:
if not ,
it shall turn to you again.
And in the same house remain,
eating and drinking such things as they give:
for the labourer is worthy of his hire.
Go not from house to house.
And into whatsoever city ye enter ,
and they receive you, eat such things as are set before you:
and heal the sick that are therein,
and say unto them,
the Kingdom of God is come nigh unto you.

Note:
Most churches have not understood the basic reason,
that God put them together as a group.
They are meant to be a training center.
In fact Jesus never encouraged anyone to build a church building.
They did have churches,
but they gathered in existing buildings or in homes.
Their churches were service centers
where people gathered mostly to pray, and to learn.

Giving thanks: Praying before we eat anything

In Canada - 20 million people are affected annually with digestive disorders
In USA - 62 million people are affected annually with digestive disorders.

I've met hundreds of Christians that seemingly just forget to pray before they eat.
People don't even realize why we pray before we eat.

1 Timothy 4:1-5
Now the Spirit speaketh expressly,
that in the latter times (that's us, the age we are in)
some shall depart from the faith,
giving heed to seducing spirits,
and doctrines of devils;
speaking lies in hypocrisy;
having their conscience seared with a hot iron;
forbidding to marry,
and commanding to abstain from meats,
which God hath created
to be received with: thanksgiving
of them which believe and know the truth.
For every creature of God is good,
    (every creature - Wow)
and nothing to be refused,
if
it be received: with thanksgiving (why)
for it is:
sanctified by: the word of God (sanctified means - cleansing, purified, made Holy)
    : and Prayer.
Note:
Therefore,
even if the food isn't really good for us
God fixes it to be wholesome for us.

Drinks are a different story.

St. Mark 16 : 16 -18
He that believeth and is baptized (into Jesus' death)
shall be saved; but he that believeth not shall be damned.

And these signs shall follow them that believe.
In my name shall they cast out devils;
They shall speak with new tongues;
They shall take up serpents;
And ***if they drink any deadly thing it shall not hurt them***;
they shall lay hands on the sick, and they shall recover.

Most churches totally miss the point of their purpose.

Most Churches miss the point
that it is Gods will
for people to activate.
To be sent out, once they are trained.
Jesus trained his disciples for three years.

Churches are to be warning centers.
Churches are to warn the outsiders,
in every city,
that if they do not repent and turn to God,
from their wicked ways,
that God will judge them
and punish them eternally with everlasting fire.

God gave us this message in :
Ezekiel 3:18-20
When I say unto the wicked,
thou shalt surely die;
and thou givest him not warning,
nor speakest to warn the wicked from his wicked way,
to save his life;
the same wicked man shall die in his iniquity;
but his blood will I require at thine hand.
Yet if thou warn the wicked,
and he turn not from his wickedness,

nor from his wicked way,
he shall die in his iniquity;
but thou hast delivered thy soul.
Again,
when a righteous man doth turn from his righteousness,
and commit iniquity,
and I lay a stumbling block before him,
he shall die:
because thou hast not given him warning,
he shall die in his sin,
and his righteousness which he hath done shall not be remembered;
but his blood will I require at thine hand.
Nevertheless
if thou warn the righteous man,
that the righteous sin not,
and he doth not sin,
he shall surely live,
because he is warned;
also thou hast delivered thy soul.
Note:
Warning is a big part of a churches responsibility.
We will be held accountable.

Today,
we all admire the huge churches for their success.
The pastors train their people and keep them,
instead of sending their people out.
And their service to all their surrounding neighbors is very limited.

*The church has not healed the sick,
because they cannot know where the sick are at home
if they don't go there.

*The church has not cured diseases.

*The church has not cast out devils.
They will not know which homes have demon possessed people

if they aren't sent out.

*The church has not warned the wicked.
They don't look for any of this in most churches.
Jesus called this loving your neighbour as yourself.

*The church has not warned the righteous who have begun to sin.
If they are not sent out, they are generally afraid to confront a church member about sin things.

I have found that it is hugely more productive to send people out in two's.
**They protect each other from sin. Why ? Because there is much more temptation*
when Christians are activated.
**There is much more power in the spirit when there are two together.*

In every church,
People are trying to figure out what their ministries are.
I tell people that what ever kind of previous problems you had
before the Lord saved you,
that is your ministry.
If you were in Jail, you have a ministry to those people.
If you had cancer, those other cancer patients are your ministry.
If you are divorced person, you should help other divorced persons.
These people become your circle of influence.

CHAPTER 15
My Sheep hear my voice

Note:
Once you are saved,
you are to work out your own salvation !

Who is talking about that?
And if so, exactly how do you do that?
The Bible is full of information,
that the sinner's prayer is only the beginning.

Philippians 2:11-13
And that every tongue should confess
That Jesus Christ is Lord,
To the glory of God the Father.
Wherefore, my beloved,
as ye have always obeyed,
not as in my presence only,
but now much more in my absence,

work out your own salvation
with fear and trembling.
For it is God which worketh in you
both to will
and to do
of his good pleasure.

Note:
It's all about doing God's good pleasure.

St. John 10:25-28
Jesus answered them,
I told you,
and ye believed me not:
the works that I do in my Father's name ,
they bear witness of me.
But
ye believed me not,
because ye are not of my sheep,
as I said unto you.
My sheep
hear my voice,
and I know them,
and they follow me;

And I give unto them
eternal life;
and they shall never perish
neither shall any man pluck them out of my hand.

Note:
It is a very simple formula.
King Jesus wanted everyone to understand it.
My sheep hear my voice,
and I know them.
How do we get King Jesus to know us.
By listening to him and obeying him.
All the time.
It's not a part time thing.
And then he says, "they follow me" .
No follow, no voice. Simple.
King Jesus will ask you to do something,
and if you don't do it,
he won't communicate with you again,
because he doesn't want to make you more disobedient.

Being in "Servant Mode" is critical to hearing his voice.
Hearing his voice is critical to following him.
Following him and bearing fruit is the objective.
Feeding your fruit sufficiently to remain, is the obligation.
Receiving what you need from the Father, is the reward.

St. John 8:47
He that is of God
heareth God's words:
ye therefore hear them not,
because
ye are not of God.

St. John 18:37
Pilate therefore said unto him,
art thou a King then?
Jesus answered.
Thou sayest that I am a king.
To this end was I born,
and for this cause came I into the world,
that I should bear witness unto the truth.
Everyone that is of the truth
heareth my voice.

Deuteronomy 28:1-2
And it shall come to pass,
If
thou shalt hearken
diligently (listen really hard, it's not easy)

1. unto the voice (this is a hearing thing)
   of the Lord thy God,
2. to observe (this is a watching thing, seeing what he is showing you)
   and
   to do all his commandments

which I command thee this day,
that the Lord thy God
will set thee on high
above all nations of the earth:
and all these blessings shall come upon thee,
and overtake thee,
if
thou shalt hearken
unto the voice
of the Lord thy God.

St. John 10:16
And
other sheep I have,
which are not of this fold:
them also
I must bring,
and they shall hear my voice;
and there shall be
one fold,
and one shepherd.

Note:
Hearing the voice of King Jesus
is not possible:
until a person has been water baptized
in "the name of the Lord Jesus",
and has received "the baptism of the Holy Ghost",
by the laying on of hands.

From the beginning
God purposed to make man
so that he could communicate with him.
He made man so that he could instruct him.
It was always Gods intention
to have man hear his voice.

But
he also set conditions.

Deuteronomy 4:36
Out of heaven he made thee to hear his voice,
that he might instruct thee:
and upon earth he showed thee his great fire;
and thou heardest his words
out of the midst of the fire.

Note:
It is not possible to be a servant to King Jesus
if you cannot hear his instruction,
and you cannot do what he tells you to do,
if you cannot hear him.
And you cannot follow him,
if you do not hear him.

Following is not the same as leading.
When King Jesus leads, great things happen.

Psalm 72:18
Blessed be the Lord God,
the God of Israel,
who only doeth wonderous things !

CHAPTER 16
"Why aren't people afraid of God?"

Note:
God controls the entire universe.
Our planet earth is 7,913 miles in diameter.
A small star near earth, "Star Betelgeuse", is 345 million miles in diameter.
Our galaxy, the Milky way, has more than one hundred billion stars.
There are more than 200 billion galaxies.
And God controls them all with his right hand .

Isaiah 48:13
Mine hand also hath laid the foundation of the earth,
and my right hand hath spanned the heavens:
when I call unto them,
they stand up together.

Note:
And God knows them all by name and number.

Isaiah 40:25-26
To whom will ye liken me,
or shall I be equal?
saith the Holy One.
Lift up your eyes on high,
and behold who hath created these things,
that bringeth out their host by number:

He calleth them all by names
by his greatness of his might,
for that he is strong in power;
not one faileth.
Note:
So, when you hear that a star has died, it is not true.
God may just have pushed another bigger star in front of it.
And he destroyed all the people of Planet earth (except Noah's family)
in the great flood, because of sin.
And he has told us he will destroy planet earth when he comes back,
but
he has built a New earth and a New heaven for his saints.
All the current stars will become the lake of fire.

All over the world people are openly offending God,
thinking that sin has no effect in their lives.
God says in: ***Ecclesiastes 8:11***
Because sentence against an evil work
is not executed speedily,
therefore, the heart of the sons of men
is fully set in them to do evil.

"***The Living Bible***" says:
Because God does not punish sinners instantly,
people feel it is safe to do wrong.

Imagine:
If every time you did even a small sin,
like thinking an evil thought,
God would send a 110-volt shock into your brain.

You would scream out in terrible pain,
and yell out to God:
I'm sorry God,
Please stop God.
I promise not to do that again.
Help me God.

Please stop.

People don't even consider the ten commandments anymore,
Such as:
- Taking His name in vain
- Keeping the Sabbath Day Holy
- Committing adultery
- Bearing false witness
- Coveting thy neighbor's things (***Exodus 20:1-7)***
- Pride
- Arrogancy
- The evil way
- The froward mouth ***(Proverbs 8:13)***
- The counsel of the ungodly
- Standing in the way of sinners
- Sitting in the seat of the scornful ***(Psalms 1:1)***

People seemingly don't appreciate
that all of their blessings
come from God.

James 1:17

Every good gift, and every perfect gift
is from above,
and cometh down from the Father of lights

From my office window, God's flashlight shining a rainbow spotlight on the mountain.
It's from above, and cometh down from the Father of lights. James 1:17
While I was writing this book, I looked up and God showed me this .
I quickly took a picture with my camera.

Deuteronomy 28:2
God says:
And all these blessings shall come on thee,
and overtake thee,
if
thou shalt hearken unto the voice
of the Lord thy God.

Psalms 128:1
Blessed is everyone that feareth the Lord;
that walketh in his ways.

Note:
So,
that would conclude:
that if a Christian doesn't have God's blessings,
the fear of the Lord and walking in God's ways,
may be currently missing.

What exactly is ***"Fear of the Lord"***

Proverbs 1:7
The fear of the Lord is:
the "beginning of knowledge"
but fools despise wisdom and instruction.

Proverbs 9:10
The fear of the Lord is:
the "beginning of wisdom"
and "the knowledge of the Holy"
is understanding.

How does this work?
Proverbs 3:7
Be not wise in thine own eyes:
fear the Lord,
and depart from evil.

Note:
So,
What is the difference?
between having fear of the Lord
and not having fear of the Lord?

Proverbs 19:23
The fear of the Lord
tendeth to life: (how?)
and he that hath it
shall abide satisfied;
he shall not be visited with evil.

Note:
That is really profound.
Everyone that takes a chance to provoke God,
by openly offending God,
is risking
the removal of Gods blessings,
and
being visited with evil.

"Fear of the Lord" is the key !

CHAPTER 17
What makes a church exciting?

Answer: When people see "God action."

Yes, real God action.
What kind of church will have real God action.
Only a Spirit filled church that operates in all of the gifts of the Holy Spirit.

Everything else is man made.
Great preaching.
Great singing.
Great churches buildings.
Great band music.
Great choirs.
Great sound systems.
Great seating.
Great prayers being said.
It's all man made.

Only when the Holy Spirit is present,
is there God action.
And if the Holy Spirit is present ,
and the people are filled with the Holy Spirit,
then the manifestation of the Holy Spirit is given in the church;
and then:
words of wisdom are spoken,
words of knowledge are spoken,
words of faith are spoken,
gifts of healing are given,
working of miracles is given,
words of prophecy are given,
discerning of spirits is given,
words of tongues are given,
words of interpretation of tongues are given,

which is what makes a church exciting !

CHAPTER 18
Operating in the Spirit.

Saint Paul made it clear to the church in Corinth.

1 Corinthians 2: 1-5
And I ,
brethren,
when I came to you,
came not with excellency of speech or in wisdom,
declaring unto you
the testimony of God.
For I determined not to know any thing among you,
save Jesus Christ,
and him crucified.
And I was with you in weakness,
and in fear,
and in much trembling.
And my speech and my preaching
was not with enticing words of man's wisdom,
but in demonstration of the Spirit and of power:
That your faith should not stand in the wisdom of men,
but in the power of God.

Note:
Once you have been baptized with the Holy Spirit,
everything changes.
You begin to understand things in the Bible

that you have never understood before.
It's because the Holy Spirit is showing you things.
The Holy Spirit works for you in every part of your life.

The Holy Spirit is also called the Comforter.
His Majesty, King Jesus, told us before he left planet earth,
that he would send us the Comforter,
and the Comforter would teach us all things.

1 John 2:27
But the anointing which ye have received of him
abideth in you,
and ye need not that any man teach you:
but as the same anointing teacheth you of all things,
and is truth,
and is no lie,
and even as it hath taught you, ye shall abide in him.

St. John 14:26
But the Comforter,
which is the Holy Ghost,
whom the Father will send in my name,
he shall teach you all things,
and bring all things to your remembrance,
whatsoever I have said unto you.

Note:
It is a wonderful feeling to be led by the Holy Spirit.
It is also wonderful to be in his presence and be guided by him.
The Holy Spirit becomes your best friend.
And when you speak in tongues in his presence,
God action happens.

The Holy Spirit knows what is the mind of the Father,
and therefore can pray perfect prayers for you
within the will of the Father.
Those prayers instantly become power prayers.

Romans 8:26 - 27
Likewise the Spirit also helpeth our infirmities:
for we know not what we should pray for as we ought:
but the Spirit itself maketh intercession for us
with groanings which cannot be uttered.
And he that searcheth the hearts
knoweth what is the mind of the Spirit,
because he maketh intercession for the saints
according to the will of God.
And we know
that all things work together for good
to them that love God,
to them who are the called
according to his purpose.
Note:
The baptism of the Holy Spirit gives us special privilege
to operate in the Spirit and not in the flesh.
Therefore Christians who have received the Holy Spirit,
need to consciously endeavor to walk in the Spirit and not in the flesh.
Operating in the Spirit
is entering into the realm of the Spirits,
and it is a realm of seeing things
that ordinary people cannot see,
and cannot experience.
To have The Holy Spirit respond to you is beyond incredible.
The feeling is exhilarating.

Romans 8:4 -9
That the righteousness of the law
might be fulfilled in us,
who walk not after the flesh,
but after the spirit.
For they that are after the flesh
do mind the things of the flesh;
but they that are after the Spirit
the things of the Spirit.

For to be carnally minded is death;
but to be spiritually minded is life and peace.
Because
the carnal mind is enmity against God:
for it is not subject to the law of God,
neither indeed can be.
So then they that are in the flesh cannot please God.
But
ye are not in the flesh,
but in the Spirit,
if so be that the Spirit of God dwell in you.
Now
if any man have not the Spirit of Christ,
he is none of his.

Note :
Even with this powerful statement of truth,
most Churches around the world
are still refusing the baptism of the Holy Spirit.

God has told us that we must worship him
in the Spirit
and in truth.
St. John 4:24
God is a Spirit:
and they that worship him
must worship him in Spirit and in truth.

Note:
It's sad that most churches
refuse to believe the entire Bible.
They say that they do,
but in reality they don't.

1 Corinthians 14:13 -15
Wherefore
let him that speaketh in an unknown tongue

pray that he may interpret.
For if I pray in an unknown tongue,
my spirit prayeth,
but my understanding is unfruitful.
What is it then?
I will pray with the Spirit,
and I will pray with the understanding also :
I will sing with the Spirit,
and I will sing with the understanding also.

Note:
When I am asked to pray for someone's healing,
I pray in English first,
and then I pray in tongues.
While praying with the Spirit (tongues)
the Holy Spirit shows me what is wrong
and what I should do.
Most of the time there are Spiritual things
that I could not have physically figured out.
I would have had no way of knowing what is really going on.
Sometimes things are simple.
Sometimes there are demons.
Sometimes there is nothing and that person is not actually sick.
Just looking for attention.
Sometimes people in wheelchairs are terrified that they might get healed.
They wouldn't know how to live if they got healed.
Their assistance would be cut off,
and their whole life would be upset.
So, they don't even want to be healed.
And the merciful Holy Spirit shows me things like that.
Demon possessed people rarely want to be healed .
Many people like their demons
even though they are being tortured by those demons.
The Holy Spirit shows me what to do,
and on occasion, has told me to be patient,

because a major war is going on
with King Jesus' angels and those demons.
Sometimes there is one demon,
like a spirit of fear,
that is causing asthma,
or headaches, or nightmares, or stomach pain.
Sometimes it is a legion of demons,
literally hundreds of them,
and it can be very dangerous for people to be in the same area.
And when those hundreds of demons come out,
they are screaming, and looking for another place to enter,
And it is dangerous.
They can go into another human,
or even into a cat or dog.
And when they are coming out of a person,
they usually torture that person on the way out.
Their can be a lot of violence.
Every situation is different.

I have never been hurt casting out a demon.
But I strongly advise that no one,
who is not a Spirit filled Christian, with a gift of discernment,
ever attempt to cast out demons.
Demons are not afraid of people.
Only the Holy Spirit can cast them out.

Prophesying is also powerful.
Word of knowledge,
Word of wisdom,
or actual Prophecy ,
are all totally contingent to having
that strong relationship with the Holy Spirit.
What most of you don't know,
is that when I have been given these things,
like a word of wisdom,
I am always in the dark as to what I am going to say.

It's that way with all prophecy
and all words of knowledge too.
You don't get the message in advance.
And afterwards you are as amazed,
as the person you gave it to.
Tongues is just letting your mouth, and tongue be loose,
and make words with out any thought to real words.
You need to make the noise, just like speaking,
but the words that come out are not yours.
What amazed me right from the start,
was that I had complete control,
as to when I start and when I stop.
At first, that made me think
that my tongues wasn't really real.
But when I minister to someone and there are manifestations,
it becomes very real, that my tongues are working.

Often, when I have my hands on someone's head,
during a healing,
I know when that person is healed,
by the amount of heat that comes into my hands.
I have no idea if anyone else, that does healings, has that same thing happen,
but for me, it's a signal from the Holy Spirit, and it's very real.
Then I merely inform the person that they are healed,
even though there may not be any other physical evidence of the healing.
But it has never failed me yet.
Sometimes the actual evidence comes sometime later,
even the next day.

Note:
When teaching the word of God,
it is very important to exactly determine "what message"
you are planting into your audience.
People only hear about twenty-five percent of what you say.

Therefore,
repeating the exact message four times during the teaching
should help them to get it.
Also remember, that less is more.

"Wisdom" is the ability to convey profound thoughts, with few words.

CHAPTER 19
Five men leading the church, to fill all things.

Ephesians 4:8 - 11
Wherefore he saith,
when he ascended up on high,
he led captivity captive and gave gifts unto men.

(Now that he ascended ,
What is it
but that he also descended first
to the lower parts of the earth?
He that descended
is the same also that ascended up
far above the heavens,
that he (Jesus) might fill all things)

Note:
Jesus Christ filled all things,
by giving the Church the "Five fold" management team.
It seems strange,
but
the word says that he gave the church these five gifts,
that he might fill all things.
That would indicate that without these five gifts,
a church is not filled and therefore only partially functional.

Verse 11:
and he gave (that's King Jesus)
some, apostles;
and some, prophets;
and some, evangelists
and some, pastors
and teachers.
Note:
These five are all very different in their calling,
but fitly joined together.
They have very different functions
and will have difficulty
if they try to do the others work.
Pastors are not evangelists,
Teachers are not Prophets,
Evangelists are not Apostles.
I have seen prophets attempt to pastor churches and fail.
They generally do this
because prophets are not paid by a congregation,
and when they have families to support,
they turn to work in the church, and usually fail.

They are not shepherds. However,
evangelists,
and prophets
and teachers,
and apostles,
are not lessor in the congregation,
and certainly not lessor than the pastor.

They all need to be equally supported.
All five are equally important to the success
and growth of the church.
These are equal full time positions in the church.

These men cannot and should not have two masters.
They should not need to have a secular job
as well as serve God in these functions.
In every church ten working people,
can support one of these ministries.

As the church grows,
this burden begins to ease.
But the church itself also has large costs.

And as the church grows,
the poor need also to be supported.
and the widows.
and the orphans.
and those that come out of prisons.
and the hungry.
and the thirsty.

Until the 1900's
the leadership and aristocracy of a church denomination
had great authority and influence
with the reigning royalty in each nation.
Then the great wars took place
and democracy started to slip in,
and take hold,
with human rights privilege.

Eventually, over the next fifty years,
Christianity no longer had much influence or authority
and Christianity began a rapid decline in every country.
For the most part,
Christianity has been the adversary of human rights.
The decline of morality and law
are the direct result.
And the clergy in every nation have totally misunderstood
the authoritative nature of their calling.
Just look at the influence

that God's men had
over the royalty in the Bible.

Several great evangelists have tried to influence presidents,
but what the media has told us,
is that generally they were merely golfing buddies of presidents.
And they have done the prayer breakfasts.
But to actually influence our world leaders in their law making,
or on morality issues has had little result.
Most politicians don't seem to be afraid of God.

CHAPTER 20
Starting a church

Without the management team in place,
God's plan cannot work.
It's starts with the five-fold ministry.

God calls these men, (God determines who they should be)
in the management team,
and gives them supernatural power
and supernatural wisdom.

1 Corinthians 1:24-29
But unto them which are called,
both Jews and Greeks,
Christ the power of God,
and the wisdom of God.
Because the foolishness of God is wiser than men;
and the weakness of God is stronger than men.

For ye see your calling, brethren,
how that not many wise men after the flesh,
not many mighty,
not many noble,
are called:

But God hath chosen the foolish things of this world
to confound the wise;

and God hath chosen the weak things of this world
to confound the things which are mighty;
And base things of the world,
and things which are despised,
hath God chosen,
yea, and things which are not,
to bring to nought things that are:
that no flesh should glory in his presence.

Romans 11:29

For the gifts and calling of God are without repentance. (irrevocable).

Note:

God does not withdraw what he has given.
And he does not change his mind about the people that he gives those gifts to.
Even if it is discovered that one these people have sinned,
God does not withdraw the gifts that He has a given to that person.

God calls people to his purpose.

Romans 8:28

And we know that all things work together for good,
to them that love God,
to them who are called according to his purpose.

Note:

When God speaks things or gifts into existence,
it happens, and he makes it good.

Numbers 23:19

God is not a man,
that he should lie;
neither the son of man,
that he should repent:
hath he said, and shall he not do it?
or hath he spoken, and shall he not make it good?

***Note*:**
From this, we understand who God will call,
to these management positions.

The Holy Spirit , (who is also King Jesus)
gave these leadership gifts for the church.
It's God's ordained management team.
God has determined this team.

CHAPTER 21
The work of God's management team

Ephesian 4:12 - 13

1. For the perfecting of the saints,
   (that means that when a church starts up
   the saints are generally not at all perfect yet,
   and they still have a long way to go,
   and much to learn.)
2. for the work of the ministry (this team of five members will train up ministers)
3. for the edifying of the body of Christ
   (edifying means to lift up, which means the congregation is going to need
   constant encouragement)
4. till we all come in the unity of the faith
   (which means that in the beginning there will not be unity of the faith.
   Lots of disagreement and many opinions of doctrine)
5. and knowledge of the Son of God
   (the church will initially not actually know King Jesus and will not be able to communicate with him. Remember, King Jesus said "my sheep hear my voice, and I know them. But the people in the church also need to know him)
6. unto a perfect man, unto the measure of the stature of the fulness of Christ

(the entire church will need to come into Holiness living, totally committed to servanthood, and totally become Christ like)

Note:
So where are the Apostles and Prophets and Evangelists today?
Some are visible.
But very few that are called by God, are evident in their calling.

One of the reasons that these actually
"God called five-fold ministers" are not recognized,
is that they probably don't have the credentials,
that current pasters get.

The ministries that God has set in the church

are written in:
1 Corinthians 12:28
And God hath set some in the church,

First apostles,
secondarily prophets,
thirdly teachers,
after that miracles,
then gifts of healings,
helps,
governments,
diversities of tongues.

Note:
The apostles are shamed into exclusion,
by the eldership of most denominations.
Most likely the apostles don't have a master's degree or a Doctorate,
and therefore the eldership consider them inferior
to a person they might consider for leadership.
Most prophets are simply denounced as false.
Evangelist quit because they run out of money.
Missionaries come home,
because eventually their sponsorship dries up.
And teachers in most denominations,
are expected to donate their time and effort.
Consequently the five-fold ministries "that God has called",
are generally unknown amongst Christians.

God created the five-fold ministry management team.
His plan is perfect in design.
It will still work perfectly today.
But people need first to recognize that it is God's plan.

Note:
But
the churches need to know
what God is going to do with this group.
God has enabled them.
They will get it done,
because it's God's plan.
They will get every joint supplying,
to the effectual working
in the measure of every part
and will make increase of the body,
until the entire church
comes into the unity of the faith,
and edify's itself in love.

CHAPTER 22
Chosen by King Jesus

The five-fold ministries

Ephesians 4:10-11

He that descended is the same also that ascended up
far above all heavens, that he might fill all things.
And he gave (that is: King Jesus gave)

1. some apostles
2. and some prophets
3. and some evangelists
4. and some pastors (shepherds)
5. and some teachers.

St. Matthew 7:15
Beware of false prophets,
which come to you in sheep's clothing,
but inwardly they are ravening wolves.

Then King Jesus also taught us how to tell the difference.
St. Matthew 7:16-17
Ye shall know them by their fruits.
Do men gather grapes of thorns,
or figs of thistles?

Even so
every good tree bringeth forth good fruit;
but a corrupt tree bringeth forth evil fruit.

Note:

The congregation will not choose the Elders and Bishops and Deacons.

The choosing of the Elders and Bishops and Deacons is done by the five fold ministry team. It is done with fasting and praying, and the Holy Spirit will separate their Elders and Bishops and Deacons.

Elders:

The prerequisites

Titus 1:5 - 9

For this cause left I thee in Crete,
that thou shouldest set in order the things that are wanting,
and ordain elders in every city,
as I had appointed thee:

1. If any be blameless (of good reputation and above reproach)
2. The husband of one wife
3. Having faithful children not accused of riot or unruly (obedient children who respect him)
4. Let the elders that rule well be counted of double honour, especially they who labour in the word and doctrine.

Note:

Elders and Bishops and Deacons are to be ordained
by the five fold ministry.

Bishops

The prerequisites of Bishops is also well documented.

1 Timothy 3:1-7 and Titus 1:7-9

1. Must be blameless (of good reputation and above reproach)
2. not soon angry,
3. not given to wine
4. no striker, not self willed

5. not greedy of filthy lucre
6. but given to hospitality
7. apt to teach, holding fast the faithful word
8. sober,
9. just
10. Holy
11. patient
12. not a brawler
13. not covetous
14. one that ruleth his own house well
15. having his children in subjection with all gravity
16. temperate (of good behaviour)
17. husband of one wife
18. Vigilant
19. Not a novice, as the steward of God
20. That he may be able by sound doctrine both to exhort and to convince the gainsayers
21. Having a good report

Deacons

The prerequisites of Deacons is well documented.

1 Timothy 3:8 -13

Likewise must the Deacons be

1. grave,
2. not double-tongued,
3. not given to much wine
4. not greedy of filthy lucre
5. holding the mystery of the faith in pure conscience
6. and let these first be proved; (trial period)
7. and let them use the office of a deacon, being found blameless
8. Even so must their wives be grave
9. Not slanderers,
10. Sober
11. Faithful in all things
12. Let deacons be the husbands of one wife

13. Ruling their children and their own houses well

The other functions in the church

- Gift of miracles
- Gifts of healings
- Helps
- Governments
- Diversities of tongues
- Those that interpret

These other functions are not operational in the church,
until the five-fold ministry sorts out what the Holy Spirit has given.
These "Gifts of the Holy Spirit" are given
when a church member accepts the Holy Spirit,
by the laying on of hands, by those five-fold members
that already have the baptism of the Holy Spirit.

Those members of the five-fold ministry
that have been given discernment,
may then sort out, who has what gifts in the church.

Then these gifts should be come evident
by the practice of these gifts.

For example,
when someone is given the gift of healing,
and lays hands on someone who needs healing,
and that person is healed,
the entire church should be made aware of this gift in their midst.

The other gifts will be discovered in the same way.

It should also become evident, who the sponsors in the church are.
God always blesses financially, some more than others.
These are people who are given the gifts of helps and governments.

Martin Luther
had an interesting comment on rich people:
"Riches" are the pettiest and least worthy gifts which God can give a man.
What are they compared to
Gods word,
to bodily gifts such as beauty and health,
or to the gifts of the mind,
such as understanding,
skill,
or wisdom.
Yet men toil for them day and night,
and take no rest.
Therefore,
God commonly give riches to foolish people,
to whom he gives nothing else.

The story of Ananias and Sapphira amplifies this.

The Acts 5:1-14
But a certain man named Ananias, with Sapphira his wife,
sold a possession,
and kept back part of the price,
his wife also being privy to it,
and brought a certain part,
and laid it at the apostles' feet.

But Peter said,
Ananias,
why hath Satan filled thine heart to lie, to the Holy Ghost,
and to keep back part of the price of the land?
Whiles it remained,
was it not thine own?
and after it was sold,
was it not in thine own power?
Why hast thou conceived this thing in thine heart?

Thou hast not lied unto men,
but unto God.
And Ananias hearing these words fell down,
and gave up the ghost:
and great fear came on all them that heard these things.
And the young men arose,
wound him up,
and carried him out,
and buried him.
And it was about the space of three hours after,
when his wife,
not knowing what was done, came in.
And Peter answered unto her,
tell me whether ye sold the land for so much?
And she said, Yea, for so much.
Then Peter said unto her,
How is it that ye have agreed together
to tempt the Spirit of the Lord?
Behold,
the feet of them which have buried thy husband
are at the door,
and shall carry thee out.
Then fell she down straightway at his feet,
and yielded up the ghost:
and the young men came in ,
and found her dead,
and,
carrying her forth,
buried her by her husband.
And great fear came upon all the church,
and upon as many as heard these things.

Note:

God has clearly instructed us how he has set up a church.
It is interesting to note that most Christians,
never realize that it is actually God that sets up a Church.

God will send just the right people
that he has called together,
to form a church.

1 Corinthians 12:28-31

And God hath set some in the church
    (Why some? Because not all of these will be added at the start.
    Some will be added later.)
first apostles,
secondarily prophets,
thirdly teachers,
after that miracles,
then gifts of healings,
helps,
governments,
diversities of tongues.

Are all apostles?
Are all prophets?
Are all teachers?
Are all workers of miracles?
Have all the gifts of healing?
Do all speak with tongues?
Do all interpret?

But
covet earnestly the best gifts:
and yet show I unto you a more excellent way.

CHAPTER 23
God's more excellent way

His plan for "Unity in the body" of Christ

God says in: ***Ephesians 4:11 -16***

And he gave some,
Apostles;
And some,
Prophets;
And some,
Evangelists;
And some,
Pastors and teachers;

(Why did he give these five management positions?)

For the perfecting of the saints,
for the work of the ministry,
for the edifying of the body of Christ:

What is the goal of this management team?

Till we all come in the unity of the faith,
and of the knowledge of the Son of God,
unto a perfect man,
unto the measure of the stature
of the fulness of Christ:

*(**Why do we need this teaching, by this management team?)***

That we henceforth be no more children,
tossed to and fro,
and carried about with every wind of doctrine,
by the sleight of men,
and cunning craftiness,
whereby they lie in wait to deceive;

But
speaking the truth in love,
may grow up into him in all things,
which is the head,
even Christ:
from whom the whole body
fitly joined together and compacted (joined together by King Jesus and compacted)
by that which every joint supplieth,
(God puts together a congregation,
where every member has something to contribute)
according to the effectual working
in the measure of every part,
maketh increase of the body (God's plan for church growth)
unto the edifying of itself in love.

Note:
This is Gods church plan.
This clearly shows the will of God.
God wishes for every joint to supply.
That is,
every person in the church has something to contribute.

God has placed each church together with specific people,
who each have a job function to fulfill in that church.

When everyone in the church is working effectually,
God says this church will have increase,
and the people will have harmony,
by everyone edifying (lifting up),
with an attitude of love.

CHAPTER 24
Christians: are definitely not perfect yet

Every Christian you have ever met, is also not a perfect Christian.
You would not believe what I discovered in my travels,
about other ministers' lives. If people knew what I saw,
many great men and women of God would lose their jobs.
I have chosen in my books, not to mention any of the faults and sins,
of other ministries. I've got enough of my own. I have not mentioned
mine either.

God has clearly told us,
In *St. Matthew 7:1*
"Judge not, that ye be not judged."

God has also clearly told us in
Romans 3:23,
"For all have sinned and come short of the glory of God".

So, when your circle of influence has someone that obviously
has not behaved the way a Christian should, it is not your job to
to judge or spread that information around.
The elders of this church should be monitoring their flock.

God is able to correct Christians. Christians are holy before God
because God has made them righteous.
Because of what King Jesus did on the Cross. He shed his blood for us,
and took our punishment on himself. We became righteous and Holy
by Jesus. But God sees everything. Christians fall into temptation.

The Bible says in
2 Peter 2:9
The Lord knoweth how to deliver the Godly
out of temptations, and to reserve the unjust unto the day of judgment
to be punished.
The lesson here, is to not let other Christian's sin
influence your view of Christianity.
There are no perfect Christians.

King Jesus also told us :
St. Matthew 18:15
Moreover if thy brother shall trespass against thee,
go and tell him his fault between thee and him alone:
if he shall hear thee, thou hast gained thy brother.

King Jesus taught us in
St. Mark 11:25
And when ye stand praying,
forgive,
if ye have ought against any:
that your father also which is in heaven
may forgive you your trespasses.
But if ye do not forgive,
neither will your father which is in heaven.
forgive your trespasses.

St. Matthew 6:9-13
Our Father, which art in heaven,
Hallowed be thy name.
Thy kingdom come.
Thy will be done in earth, as it is in heaven.
Give us this day our daily bread.
And forgive us our debts, ***(our sins - St. Luke 11:4)***
as we forgive our debtors.
And lead us not into temptation,
but deliver us from evil:

For thine is the kingdom,
and the power,
and the glory,
for ever, Amen.

Christian's sin. Just forgive them.

CHAPTER 25
Abiding in the Vine

Abiding in the vine is not optional.
If every person in a church were abiding in the vine,
that church would be more than triple in size, every few months.
The Bible says we will have much fruit,
if we abide in the vine.
How much do you think "much" is.
You've been around fruit trees.
How much is much on one branch?

St. John 15:1- 8

I am the true vine,
and my Father is the husbandman.
Every branch in me that beareth not fruit
he taketh away:
and every branch that beareth fruit,
he purgeth it,
that it may bring forth more fruit.
Now ye are clean through the word
which I have spoken to you.
Abide in me,
and I in you.
As the branch cannot bear fruit of itself,
except it abide in the vine;
no more can ye,

except ye abide in me.
I am the vine,
ye are the branches:
He that abideth in me,
and I in him,
the same bringeth forth much fruit:
for without me ye can do nothing.
If a man abide not in me,
he is cast forth as a branch,
and is withered;
and men gather them,
and cast them into the fire:
and they are burned.
If ye abide in me,
and
my words abide in you,
ye shall ask what ye will,
and it shall be done unto you.

Herein is my Father glorified
That ye bear much fruit;
So shall ye be my disciples.

Question: What is the best way to abide in the vine?

Simple.
Don't cheat on Jesus.
Don't play both sides. (Satan's side and Jesus side.)
Do all the right things.
Pray before you eat.
Talk holy conversation. Stuff that is edifying. Lifting up.
All your words are being recorded.

St. Matthew 12:36-37
But I say unto you,
that every idle word that men speak,
they shall give account thereof

in the day of Judgment.
For by thy words thou shalt be justified,
and by thy words
thou shalt be condemned

Revelation 20:12 -13
And I saw the dead.
small and great,
stand before God;
and the books were opened:
and another book was opened,
which is the "Book of Life"
and the dead were judged out of those things
which were written in the books,
according to their works.

And the sea gave up the dead which were in it ;
and death and hell delivered up the dead which
were in them:
and they were judged
every man "according to their works".
Note:
Make sure that all the things you do each day
have Jesus in priority. It's the only thing that counts.
Walk in the Spirit.
Pray about everything.

Proverbs 3:5-6
Trust in the Lord with all your heart.
Lean not to your own understanding.
In all your ways acknowledge him,
and he will direct your paths.

Of course you cannot be bearing fruit
if you sit in your house.
It's a going out thing. (***St. John 15:16***)
Walking in the spirit.

And then you need to watch
who God is bringing to you.
And then you need to approach that person
and lead him to salvation.
Being a good listener really helps.

It's all about Fruit. (leading people to salvation)

Psalms 1:1-3
Blessed is the man
that walketh not in the counsel of the ungodly,
nor standeth in the way of sinners,
nor sitteth in the seat of the scornful.
But
his delight is in "the law of the Lord"
and in his law doth he "meditate day and night".
And he shall be like a tree
planted by the rivers of water,
that bringeth forth his fruit in his season;
his leaf also shall not wither;
and whatsoever he doeth shall prosper.

1 Colossians 1: 5-6
For the hope
which is laid up for you
in heaven,
whereof ye heard before
in the word of truth of the gospel;
which is come unto you,
as it is in all the world;
(and bringeth forth fruit)
as it doth also in you,
since the day ye heard of it,
and knew the grace of God in truth.

Note:
Only two things happen:

St. John 15:6 - 8
King Jesus said :
If a man abide not in me,
he is cast forth as a branch,
and is withered;
and men gather them,
and cast them into the fire,
and they are burned.

Or

If ye abide in me,
and my words abide in you (He expects you to memorize verses)
ye shall ask what ye will,
and it shall be done unto you.
Herein is my Father glorified,
that ye bear much fruit;
so shall ye be my disciples !

Note:
When you talk to someone anywhere,
you can always tell at what level their Christianity is at,
by what they talk about.

You can also tell by this if they are in the vine !
St. Luke 6:45
A good man out of the good treasure of his heart
bringeth forth that which is good;
and an evil man out of the evil treasure of his heart
bringeth forth that which is evil:
for of the abundance of the heart, his mouth speaketh.

CHAPTER 26
King Jesus gave us three new commandments.

It is written:
St. Mark 12:29-30
And Jesus answered him,
The first of all commandments is,
Hear, O Israel;
The Lord our God is one Lord:
And thou shalt love the Lord thy God
with all thy heart,
with all thy soul,
and with all thy mind,
and with all thy strength:
this is the first commandment. (Please read ***Deuteronomy 6:5-9***)

It is written:
St. Mark 12:31
And the second is like,
namely this,
Thou shalt love thy neighbour as thyself.
There is none other commandment greater than these.
Note:
Does anyone actually care that their neighbour is going to hell?

It is written:
St. John 13:34-35
A new commandment I give unto you,
That ye love one another;
as I have loved you,
that ye also love one another.
By this shall all men know
that ye are my disciples,
if ye have love one to another.

Is it really obvious to outsiders,
that you are His Majesty's disciples?

My Friend

My friend, I stand in "the judgment" now,
and feel that you're to blame somehow.

On earth, I walked with you day by day
and never did you show me "the way".

You knew the Lord, in truth and glory ,
but never did you tell me the story.

My knowledge then was very dim ;
you could have led me safe to Him .

Though we lived together on the earth ,
you never told me of this second birth,
and now I stand this day condemned,
because you failed to mention Him !

We worked by day and talked by night,
and yet you showed me not "the light" .

You let me live, and love, and die,
and you knew I'd never live "on high"

Yes, I called you my friend in life ,
and trusted you through joy and strife .

And yet in coming to this horrible end
can I now call you "my friend" ?

CHAPTER 27
The Homeless Children
2.5 million just in the U.S.A.

The next generation is more discriminating.
In most cases their parents are no help.
They haven't even been good parents.
But these same parents cry every night for their lost children.
It's horrible.
They don't know what to do.
They don't turn to Christians,
because the Christians have not reached out to them
and told them there is hope.
God can do something.
But they don't know that.

Even 2500 years ago people had the same problem.

Lamentations 2:19
Arise
cry out in the night:
in the beginning of the watches
pour out thine heart like water before the face of the Lord:
lift up thy hands toward him
for the life of thy young children,
that faint for hunger in the top of every street.

Note:

Even their parents expressed that the "Christians on TV" are mostly phony.
And look at all the trouble many denominations are in.
Some have actually destroyed their integrity.
Who wants to send their kids to be alter boys now?
So, where does that leave this next generation?
It leaves them with no desire to even consider Christianity.
What do they do now?

Children are living in the streets.
Children are living in tents beside the highways.
Children are starving.
Children are turning to drugs.
Children are rebellious.
Children turn to crime.
Children no longer have any goals.

Many hide in drugs.
In the USA the stats for "drug overdose" deaths are :
2017 - 70,237
2018 - 67,367
2019 - 70,630
2020 - 91,799
2021 - 108,000
2022 - 110,000

Then there is alcohol abuse.
July 18, 2022 – the stats showed - 13,000,000 young people 26 or older are alcoholics.
414,000 age 12-17 had "alcohol abuse disorder"

50 percent of children under 20 have divorced parents.
It really affects their behaviour.
These kids are lost.

There are about 2.5 million homeless children in the USA today.
There are about 443,000 children in Foster care in the U.S.A.

But there is a movement of Christian young people,
who can actually reach this lost generation.

God cares about children. A lot.

It is every Christian's obligation
to reach out to these children in their neighbourhood,
and bring them hope.

St. Matthew 25:43-46
I was a stranger ,
and ye took me not in:
naked, and ye clothed me not:
sick, and in prison,
and ye visited me not.
Then shall they also answer him,
saying, Lord, when saw we thee an hungred,
or athirst, or a stranger,
or naked, or sick,
or in prison, and did not minister unto thee?
Then shall he answer them, saying,
Verily I say unto you,
inasmuch as ye did it not to one of the least of these ,
ye did it not to me.
And these shall go away into everlasting punishment:
but the righteous into life eternal.

The Holy Bible is not a book of suggestions.

When these street people are brought into your church,
don't treat them with disdain.
King Jesus looks at these lost teenagers and young people as little children.
Why? Because they know nothing about God.
They are green. Ripe for teaching.
St. Matthew 19: 14
But Jesus said,
Suffer the little children, and forbid them
not, to come unto me:
for of such is the Kingdom of Heaven.

CHAPTER 28

Heaven is magnificent
Heaven is marvellous.
Heaven is huge.

Yes, Heaven is huge.

And there will be a new city in heaven.

And this city will also be huge.

King Jesus has prepared a new city for us.
It will be called "the Holy Jerusalem"
It is huge.
It is 1500 miles long.
It is 1500 miles wide.
It has twelve stories high.
Each story is 125 miles apart.
It's hard to imagine a city twelve stories high.
And each one of us has a mansion in that new city.
And King Jesus has created a new earth.
And King Jesus has created new heavens. (a whole new set of stars and galaxies.)
And there is no death in heaven.
And there is no sickness in heaven.
And everyone gets a new spirit body in heaven.
Actually, we get this new body on our way up to heaven,
when we rise up into the clouds to meet His Majesty, King Jesus.

Revelation: 21:1-3
And I saw a new heaven and a new earth:
For the first haven and the first earth were passed away.
And there was no more sea. (The oceans are gone too)

Note:
Many bible teachers say that Jesus is coming back
to reign on this planet.
That is not true, because our current planet earth
will be melted with fervent heat
and will become part of that lake of fire.
In Jerusalem, people pay huge money to be buried near the Mount of Ascension,
at the top of the Kidron Valley, because they have been told that this is where King Jesus, the Messiah will return. It's simply not true.

Revelation 21:2-3
And I John saw the Holy City,
New Jerusalem, coming down from God out of heaven,
prepared as a bride adorned for her husband.
And I heard a great voice out of heaven saying,
Behold, the tabernacle of God is with men,
and he will dwell with them,
and they shall be his people,
and God himself shall be with them,
and be their God.

Revelation 21:10–17
And he carried me away in the Spirit
to a great and high mountain,
and showed me that great city,
the Holy Jerusalem, descending out of heaven from God,
having the glory of God:
and her light was like unto a stone most precious,
even like a jasper stone,
clear as crystal;

and had a wall great and high,
and had twelve gates,
and at the gates twelve angels,
and names written thereon,
which are the names of
the twelve tribes of the children of Israel:
on the east three gates;
on the north three gates;
on the south three gates;
and on the west three gates.
And the wall of the city had twelve foundations,
and in them the names of the twelve apostles of the Lamb.
And he that talked with me
had a golden reed to measure the city,
and the gates thereof,
and the wall thereof.
And the city lieth foursquare,
and the length is as large as the breadth:
as he measured the city with the reed,
twelve thousand furlongs.
The length and the breadth and the height of it are equal.
And he measured the wall thereof,
an hundred and forty and four cubits,
according to the measure of a man,
that is, of the angel.

Imagine, you are there!

Imagine that you have just made it to the new earth.
You have been through the famine, and pestilence, and war, and those locusts,
that sting people with their tails, those people, that didn't have His Majesty's seal in their forehead.
Then it got dark, and the earth shook,
and suddenly there was fire everywhere,

and people were getting burnt.
And then you saw His Majesty on a white horse,
and you, and people all around you, were starting to go up .
And you weren't even afraid !
And then everyone looked the same, in their new Spirit bodies.
And quick as lightning, you were being transported to this new place called the "New Earth" .
And you all stood there, before His Majesty.
And then he said , "Look over there".
And you saw it for the first time, coming down from God .
It was huge .
There were huge things back on the old earth, but nothing like this.
Fifteen hundred miles long. Fifteen hundred miles wide.
Fifteen hundred miles high . And it was still in the air.
And coming down slowly.
Something this big would have knocked the balance of planet earth, right off of it's axis, and out of it's orbit.
But then the old earth was only 7,913 miles in diameter.
They haven't told you yet, but this new earth may be several million miles in diameter.
It seems to take a long time to land, but no one is bothered about time.
It is so fascinating. And shiny.
Then his big voice says to all of you,
"we are going to take you all,
on a tour of this great "Holy City" - "New Jerusalem".
And you can hardly wait.
Imagine – twelve levels, each 125 miles apart.
And each level is fifteen hundred miles by fifteen hundred miles.
And then he showed you all, the magnificent mansions, that he had promised .
On the old earth, great mansions were the design
of great architect's wisdom.
God has said that man's wisdom is foolishness to him.
These mansions are "way beyond awesome" !

CHAPTER 29
Must worship him in Spirit and in truth

It is common in most traditional churches, to sing the old songs in a hymn book.
Those are religious traditional songs, that are mostly boring,
and don't always subscribe to Bible accuracy.

It is also common in non-denominational churches to sing songs that have been written by current artists. And the routine regiment in these churches is to sing one of these modern songs with a group of six to ten singers on stage with guitars and an electric piano behind them. The girls sing with enthusiasm and everyone on stage also dances.
It's very entertaining. And our grandmothers would be in shock and disgraced at both the form of dancing and the dress code.

Many of those songs, although well intentioned, are biblically incorrect.
And most of them are difficult to memorize.
So that the congregation cannot take the song home with them.
When these songs are sung, they are most frequently repeated many times in succession. That also becomes boring.

I was invited to preach in a "Church of Marthoma" in Calcutta.
The "Mar Thoma churches" are all over the world. The one in India was started in 52 AD by Saint Thomas. They spent hours before the service on carpets, kneeling and worshipping, and praying in tongues, and praying in Bengali, and also some singing.

Sometimes they were on their knees, sometimes they were prostrate. Sometimes they were cross legged as only they can do. (I cannot sit cross-legged at all.)
There was much sincere weeping before the Lord. The singing was with awesome reverence. It was Holy. And it was from the heart. And the Holy Spirit was vividly there.

I was also in an all-black church in Oklahoma City, which had a young white pastor,
that was very similar to a church of Mar Thoma.

My point is, that it was singing and worship directly to God.
It was not entertainment. It was from their heart.

His Majesty, King Jesus was very clear;

St. Matthew 21:13
And he said unto them,
it is written,
my house shall be called the house of prayer;
But
ye have made it a den of thieves.

Church has become a very good business.

Songs to sing in Churches

* They must line up with the Bible.
* They may be taken from Psalms and Hymns.
* They should be easy to memorize
so that people can sing these songs at home as well.

St. John 4:23-24
But the hour cometh,
and now is,
when the true worshippers
shall worship the Father
in spirit and in truth:

for the Father seeketh such to worship him.
God is a Spirit:
and they that worship him
must worship him
in spirit and in truth.

Worshipping him in spirit is singing and praying in tongues.
Worshipping him in truth is singing and praying Bible verses.

St. John 17:17
Sanctify them through thy truth:
Thy word is truth.

Songs from Bible verses

1. Thy loving kindness
2. Whoso offereth praise
3. The joy of the Lord
4. Great is the Lord
5. Thou art my God and I will praise thee
6. Thou art worthy
7. Create in me a new heart
8. From the rising of the sun
9. God gives you beauty for ashes
10. This is my commandment
11. God hath not , given to us
12. My Lord is able
13. It's no longer I that liveth
14. This is the day
15. Bless the Lord
16. Blessing, glory, and honour
17. My Yoke is easy
18. Praise ye the Lord

1. Thy loving Kindness

Psalms 63:3-4

Thy loving kindness is better than life
thy loving kindness is better than life
my lips shall praise thee
thus will I bless thee
I will lift up
my hands
in thy name

2. Whoso offereth praise

Psalms 50:23

Whoso offereth praise glorifieth me
whoso offereth praise glorifieth me
and to him that ordereth
his conversation aright
will I show the salvation of God

3. The joy of the Lord

Nehemiah 8:10

The joy of the Lord is my strength
the joy of the Lord is my strength
the joy of the Lord is my strength
Oh, the joy of the Lord is my strength.

4. Great is the Lord

Psalms 48:1-2

Great is the Lord and greatly to be praised
in the city of our God
in the mountain of his holiness
beautiful for situation
is the joy of the whole earth
is Mount Zion on the sides of the north,
the city of the great King
is Mount Zion on the sides of the north
the city of the great King.

5. Thou art my God and I will praise thee

Psalms 118:28-29

Thou art my God and I will praise thee
thou art my God and I exalt thee,
O give thanks unto the Lord
for he is good
and his mercy endureth for ever

6. Thou art worthy O Lord

Revelation 4:11

Thou art worthy
thou are worthy
thou art worthy, O Lord
thou art worthy
to receive glory
glory and honour and power.

For thou hast created
hast all things created
for thou has created all things
and for thy pleasure
they are created
thou art worthy O Lord.

7. Create in me a clean heart, O God

Psalms 51:10-11

Create in me a clean heart
O God
and renew a right spirit within me.
Create in me a clean heart
O God,
and renew a right spirit within me
Cast me not away from the presence;
and take not thy Holy Spirit from me
restore unto me
the joy of thy salvation;
and renew a right spirit within me.

8. From the rising of the Sun

Psalms 113:3……Psalms 113:1 …….. Psalms 113:2

From the rising of the sun
to the going down of the same
the Lord's name
is to be praised.

From the rising of the sun
to the going down of the same
the Lord's name is to be praise.

Praise ye the Lord
praise O ye servants of the Lord
praise ye the name of the Lord
praise ye the Lord.
praise O ye servants of the Lord
praise the name of the Lord.

Blessed be the name of the Lord
from this time forth
and forever more,
blessed be the name of the Lord
from this time forth
and forever more.

9. God gives you beauty for ashes

Isaiah 61:3

God gives you beauty for ashes
the oil of Joy for mourning
the garment of praise
for the spirit of heaviness
that we might
be called trees of righteousness
the planting of the Lord
that he might be glorified.

10. This is my commandment

St. John 15:11-12

This is my commandment
that ye love one another
that your joy might be full.

This is my commandment
that ye love one another
that your joy might be full.

That your joy might be full
that your joy might be full
This is my commandment
that ye love one another
that your joy might be full.

11. God has not given to us

2 Timothy 1:7
God has not
given to us
the Spirit of fear,
God has not given to us
the Spirit of fear,
God has not
given to us
the Spirit of fear,
but of Love,
and of Power,
and a sound mind.

12. My Lord is able

Psalms 147:3
Isaiah 42:7
Isaiah 61:1
St. Mark 4 : 39

My Lord is able
he's able
I know he is able
I know my Lord is able
to carry me through

My Lord is able
he's able
I know he is able
I know my Lord is able
to carry me through.

He heals the broken hearted
he sets the captives free
he raises dead to life again
and calms the troubled sea,
I know he's able
he's able
I know he is able
I know my Lord is able
to carry me through.

13. It's no longer I that liveth

Galatians 2:20

It's no longer I that liveth
but Christ that liveth in me
It's no longer I that liveth
but Christ that liveth in me.
He Lives
he lives
Jesus is alive in me
It is no longer I that liveth
but Christ that liveth in me.

14. This is the day

Psalms 118:24

This is the day
this is the day
that the Lord hath made
that the Lord hath made
we will rejoice
we will rejoice
and be glad in it
and be glad in it
this is the day that the Lord hath made
we will rejoice and be glad in it
this is the day
this is the day
that the Lord hath made.

15. Bless the Lord, O my soul

Psalms 103:1
Psalms 126:3

Bless the Lord,
O my soul
and all that is within me
bless his holy name.

Bless the Lord
O my soul
and all that is within me
bless his holy name.

For he hath done great things
he hath done great things
he hath done great things
bless his holy name.

16. Blessing ,Glory ,and Honour

Revelation 7:12

Blessing, glory, and honour,
power and love and dominion,
be unto thee
my precious Lord.

Blessing, glory, and honour,
power and love and dominion,
be unto thee
my precious Lord.

Coming down from your throne on high
you died on the cross for me
rising up from the grave you rose
to give me the victory
O
blessing, glory, and honour,
power and love and dominion,
be unto thee
my precious Lord.

17. My yoke is easy

St. Matthew 11:28-30
All ye that labour
come unto me
if you're heavy laden
come unto me
take my yoke upon you
and learn what's best
I am meek and lowly
and I will give you rest.

My yoke is easy
and my burden is light
my yoke is easy
and my burden is light
if you're doing it the hard way
who do you think that's from
my yoke is easy
and my burden is light.

18. Praise ye the Lord

Psalms 150:1-6

Praise ye the Lord.
Praise God in his sanctuary:
praise him in the firmament
of his power.
Praise him for his mighty acts:
praise him according
praise him according to his excellent greatness.
Praise him with the sound of the trumpet:
praise him with the psaltery and harp.
Praise him with the timbrel and dance:
praise him with stringed instruments and organs.
Praise him with the loud sounding cymbals:
praise him with the high sounding cymbals.
Let everything that hath breath praise the Lord.
Praise ye the Lord.

SONGS NOT FROM BIBLE VERSES

Table of Contents for suggested songs

1. He paid a debt he did not owe
2. I have decided to follow Jesus
3. Oh How I love Jesus
4. What a friend we have in Jesus
5. Learning to Lean
6. I'm so glad that Jesus set me free
7. It is no secret what God can do
8. How great thou art
9. Because he lives, I can face tomorrow
10. God is so good
11. For he is Lord, he is Lord
12. Making melody in your heart, unto the king of kings.
13. O come let us adore him
14. To get a touch from the Lord is so real
15. This little light of mine
16. He love us with an everlasting love
17. Amen, Amen, Amen.

1.
He paid a debt he did not owe

He paid a debt he did not owe
I owed a debt I could not pay
I needed someone to wash my sins away
and now I sing a brand new song
amazing grace all day long
Christ Jesus paid a debt
that I could never pay.

2.
I have decided to follow Jesus

I have decided
to follow Jesus
I have decided
to follow Jesus
I have decided
to follow Jesus
no turning back
no turning back

Though none go with me
still I will follow
Though none go with me
still I will follow
Though none go with me
still I will follow
no turning back
no turning back.

The cross before me
the world behind me
The cross before me
the world behind me.
The cross before me
the world behind me
no turning back
no turning back.

3.

O, how I love Jesus

Therc is a name I love to hear
I love to sing it's worth
it sounds like music to my ear
the sweetest name on earth.

Oh, how I love Jesus
Oh, how I love Jesus
Oh, how I love Jesus
because he first loved me.

It tells me of a Saviours love,
who died to set me free
it tells me of his precious blood
the sinners perfect plea.

4.

What a friend we have in Jesus

What a friend we have in Jesus
all our sins and griefs to bear
What a privilege to carry
everything to God in prayer
O what peace we often forfeit
O what needless pain we bear
All because we do not carry
everything to God in prayer.

Have we trials and temptations?
Is there trouble anywhere?
We should never be discouraged
take it to the Lord in prayer
Can we find a friend so faithful
who will all our sorrows share
Jesus knows our every weakness
take it to the Lord in prayer.

5.
Learning to lean on Jesus

Learning to lean
Learning to lean
I'm learning to lean on Jesus
finding more power than I've ever dreamed
I'm learning to lean on Jesus

6.
I'm so glad that Jesus set me free

I'm so glad that Jesus set me free
I'm so glad that Jesus set me free
I'm so glad that Jesus set me free
I'm singing glory halleluyah,
Jesus set me free.

I was bound in sin
but Jesus set me free
I was bound in sin
but Jesus set me free
I was bound in sin,
but Jesus set me free
I'm singing Glory hallelujah
Jesus set me free

7.
It is no secret what God can do

It is no secret
what God can do
what he's done for others
he will do for you
with arms wide open
he'll carry you through
it is no secret
what God can do.

8. How great thou art

O Lord, my God
when I, in awesome wonder
consider all, the worlds thy hands have made
I see the stars,
I hear the rolling thunder
thy power throughout, the universe displayed.

Then sings my soul,
my Saviour God to thee
how great thou art,
how great thou art
Then sings my soul, my Saviour God to thee
how great thou art,
how great thou art.

And when I think
that God
his Son not sparing
sent him to die,
I scarce can take it in
That on the cross,
my burden gladly bearing
he bled and died to take away my sin

Then sings my soul,
my Saviour God to thee
how great thou art,
how great thou art,
Then sings my soul,
my Saviour God to thee,
how great thou art,
how great thou art.

When Christ shall come,
with shout of acclamation

and take me home,
what joy shall fill my heart.
Then I shall bow, in humble adoration,
and then proclaim, my God, how great thou art.

Then sings my soul,
my Saviour God to thee,
how great thou art,
how great thou art.

9.
Because he lives, I can face tomorrow

Because he lives,
I can face tomorrow,
because he lives ,
all fear is gone,
because I know, I know
he holds the future
and life is worth the living
just because he lives.

10.
God is so good

God is so good,
God is so good,
God is so good,
he is good to me.

And I love him so,
and I love him so,
I love him so,
he's so good to me.

His son died for me
his son died for me
his son died for me,
he's so good to me.

11.
For he is lord

For he is Lord
He is Lord
He has risen from the dead
and he is Lord
every knee shall bow,
every tongue confess,
that Jesus Christ is Lord.

12.
Making melody in your heart

Making melody in your heart,
making melody in your heart,
making melody in your heart,
unto the King of Kings.
Worship and adore him
worship and adore him
making melody in your heart,
unto the King of Kings

13.
O come let us adore him,

O come let us adore him,
O come let us adore him,
O come let us adore him,
Christ the Lord.

We'll give him all the glory,
we'll give him all the glory,
we'll give him all the glory,
Christ the Lord.

14.
He loves us with an everlasting love

He loves us
with an everlasting love
he loves us with an everlasting love
he love us so much
that he gave us his Son
and that's
an everlasting love.

15.
This little light of mine
St. Matthew 5:15-16

This little light of mine,
I'm going to let it shine,
This little light of mine,
I'm going to let it shine,
let it shine,
let it shine,
let it shine.

Hide it under a bushel, no
I'm going to let it shine,
Hide it under a bushel, no
I'm going to let it shine,
let it shine,
let it shine,
let it shine,

Let it shine till Jesus comes,
I'm going to let it shine,
let it shine till Jesus comes,
I'm going to let it shine,
let it shine,
let it shine,
let it shine.

16.

To get a touch from the Lord is so real
James 4:8

To get a touch from
the Lord is,
so real
To get a touch from
the Lord is,
so real
If you draw nigh to him,
he will draw nigh to you,
to get a touch from
the Lord is
so real.

Halleluuuuyah
Halleluuuuyah,
Jesus is coming,
he's coming again
Halleluuuuyah
Halleluuuuyah
Jesus is coming again.

17.
Amen

Amen, Amen, Amen, Amen, Amen
Sing it over,
Amen, Amen, Amen,
Amen, Amen

See the baby,
wrapped in the manger,
on Christmas morning,
Amen, Amen, Amen.

See him in the temple,
talkin' with the elders,
who marvelled at his wisdom,
Amen, Amen, Amen.

Down at the Jordon,
where John was baptizing,
saving all sinners,
Amen, Amen, Amen.

See him at the seaside,
talkin' with the fishermen,
and making them disciples,
Amen, Amen, Amen.

Marching in Jerusalem,
over palm branches,
in pomp and splendor,
Amen, Amen, amen.

See him in the garden,
praying to his Father,
in deepest sorrow,
Amen, Amen, Amen.

Led before Pilate,
then they crucified him,
but He rose on Easter
Amen, Amen, Amen.

Hallelujah, Amen,
He died to save us,
Amen and he lives forever
Amen, Amen, Amen.

Hallelujah,
Amen, Amen, Amen

You can watch YouTube ***"Lily's of the field - Amen"***
to hear Sydney Portier sing this song.
It is a wonderful movie for the whole family.

The Bible says in :

1 Corinthians 14: 13 -15

Wherefore let him that speaketh in an unknown tongue pray that he may interpret.
For if I pray in an unknown tongue, my
spirit prayeth, but my understanding is unfruitful.
What is it then? I will pray with the Spirit,
and I will pray with understanding also:
I will sing with the spirit, and I will sing with the understanding also.

Colossians 3: 16

Let the word of Christ dwell in you richly in all wisdom;
teaching and admonishing one another
in Psalms and hymns and spiritual songs,
singing with grace in your hearts to the Lord.

Ephesians 5: 19

Speaking to yourselves in Psalms and hymns and spiritual songs,
singing and making melody in your heart to the Lord.

Questions
(to God)
Ronald F. Peters
VOLUME 1: The Mystery of Life after Death

Questions to God ,Volume 1
The mystery of life after death

Every persons current body will die. We just don't know exactly when we are leaving. So, where do people go right after they die? What is it like in the next world? What do we need to do, to have a really super life in the other world? Some ecologists, scientists and theologians believe that the earth is beginning to expire and that humans will need to leave this world, possibly in this century. The Bible tells us exactly how it is going to end. Everyone is going to live many trillions of years, after we leave. The time we spend in our current container, is preparation time for the next world. How are we to prepare, to live in our new Spirit bodies? This is a fascinating book. It is perfect for Christian Bible Studies. The entire book is written in "Question and Answer" format.

Questions
(to God)
Ronald F. Peters
VOLUME 2: The Actual Doctrine of King Jesus

Questions to God , Volume 2
The Actual Doctrine of King Jesus

The Christian Holy Bible says there are two baptisms. Nicodemus was told in St. John 3:5 "except a man be born of water and of the Spirit, he cannot enter into the Kingdom of God." There is water baptism, and the baptism of the Holy Spirit. What makes them both very important? God made two contracts with earth people, called covenants. What has changed in the second contract? These contracts are only valid and legal, if they are officially accepted. Today, we accept contracts with an official signature. The first contract was accepted by circumcision. If a male wasn't circumcised, he did not have a valid contract with God. How is the second covenant to be accepted and validated? When King Jesus left planet earth, and knowing that he was leaving for many centuries, what five things did he instruct us to do? Is God flexible, and is he democratic? How does God want us to be involved with politics? You'll be amazed at what God actually says.

Questions
(to God)
Ronald F. Peters
VOLUME 3: My Sheep Hear my Voice

Questions to God, Volume 3
My Sheep hear my voice

God said, out of heaven he made thee to hear his voice, that he might instruct thee. God said, if thou shalt hearken diligently unto the voice of the Lord thy God, to observe and to do all his commandments which I command thee this day, that the Lord thy God will set thee on high above all nations of the earth: and all these blessings shall come on thee, and overtake thee, if thou shalt hearken unto the voice of the Lord thy God. His majesty King Jesus said , My sheep hear my voice, and I know them, and they follow me. Being in servant mode, is critical to hearing his voice. Hearing his voice is critical to following him. Following him and bearing fruit is the objective. Feeding your fruit sufficiently to remain, is the obligation. Receiving what you need from the Father, is the reward. This book will show you how.

Questions
(to God)
Ronald F. Peters
VOLUME 4: Messed Up Families

Questions to God , Volume 4
Messed up Families

Grounded in scripture and addressing the critical issues facing families today, Questions to God, Volume 4 provides readers with insight and teaching that will help them and their families navigate through their "messes" and move back into the will of God.

Ronald Peters begins his book with a thorough overview of the "Stats and facts" about the mess society is in, demonstrating the need for healing from God. He addresses the thirteen commandments - ten given to Moses and three given by Jesus and the Biblical teaching on men, women, marriage, parenting, finances, the end times, and more.

Posing questions and answering with pertinent scripture passages, he provides readers with the framework for "life and that more abundantly. (St. John 10:10)

Accessible, easy to follow, and overflowing with the Word of God, Questions to God, Volume 4 will challenge, inspire, and renew.

Amazing
Missionary
Adventures

What is it really like
to be a missionary

Amazing Missionary Adventures

From a state of rebellion against God to a life devoted to full-time ministry, Ronald Peters has walked an incredible path of faith. In "Amazing Missionary Adventures" he takes the readers on a journey from British Columbia to Egypt, Hawaii, Fiji, Tonga, India, New Zealand and numerous other locations, as he chronicles his experiences answering God's call and sharing His Word.

Mr. Peters ministry has been marked by miracles, healings and clear messages from God that direct him in his travels. Readers will meet a variety of people who over the years were all touched by the Holy Spirit through the author. An inspirational book that will bolster the faith of even the most doubtful, "Amazing Missionary Adventures" is a testament to the power and faithfulness of God.

Many of you will have questions.
Some will want to debate this book.
Some will agree with what the Bible says.

Whatever your stance, contact me.
Your comments will be appreciated.
Many thanks,
Ron Peters
ronaldfpeters@gmail.com

Ronald F. Peters

Ron and Isobel are both in good health.
They have two sons that are both married,
and they are thrilled with their little grand daughter.
They live near Vancouver, British Columbia, in Canada.

Printed in the USA
CPSIA information can be obtained
at www.ICGtesting.com
JSHW071714131023
49866JS00006B/19